Small Talk

People Skills & Communication Skills You Need To Be Charismatic

(Make Real Friends, Stop Anxiety and Increase Self-Confidence)

Scott Arnott

Published By **Chris David**

Scott Arnott

All Rights Reserved

Small Talk: People Skills & Communication Skills You Need To Be Charismatic (Make Real Friends, Stop Anxiety and Increase Self-Confidence)

ISBN 978-1-77485-573-7

No part of this guidebook shall be reproduced in any form without permission in writing from the publisher except in the case of brief quotations embodied in critical articles or reviews.

Legal & Disclaimer

The information contained in this ebook is not designed to replace or take the place of any form of medicine or professional medical advice. The information in this ebook has been provided for educational & entertainment purposes only.

The information contained in this book has been compiled from sources deemed reliable, and it is accurate to the best of the Author's knowledge; however, the Author cannot guarantee its accuracy and validity and cannot be held liable for any errors or omissions. Changes are periodically made to this book. You must consult your doctor or get professional medical advice before using any of the suggested remedies, techniques, or information in this book.

Upon using the information contained in this book, you agree to hold harmless the Author from and against any damages, costs, and expenses, including any legal fees potentially resulting from the application of any of the information provided by this guide. This disclaimer applies to any damages or injury caused by the use and application, whether directly or indirectly, of any advice or information presented, whether for breach of contract, tort, negligence, personal injury, criminal intent, or under any other cause of action.

You agree to accept all risks of using the information presented inside this book. You need to consult a professional medical practitioner in order to ensure you are both able and healthy enough to participate in this program.

TABLE OF CONTENTS

Introduction 1

Chapter 1: Conversation As A Skill And Art 3

Chapter 2: The Psychological Benefits Of Small Talk...................................... 9

Chapter 3: Strategies For Small Talk Conversations 26

Chapter 4: What Is Small Talk Important? 44

Chapter 5: The Potential And Importance Of Small Talks.. 49

Chapter 6: Talking To Anyone And Feeling At Home... 59

Chapter 7: The Best Ways To Engage Women We Do Not Know 63

Chapter 8: Being Open 75

Chapter 9: Minimal Talk For People Who Aren't... 81

Chapter 10: Tip To Achieving Success In Small Talk... 90

Chapter 11: Talk The Talk 110

Chapter 12: Learn To End Any Conversation The Power Of No 123

Chapter 13: Reassurances To Self-Confidence And Confidence 127

Chapter 14: Have Fun, People Love Jokes However, Don't Overdo It. 130

Chapter 15: Small Talk Society 132

Chapter 16: What You Can Do To Enhance Your Charisma 136

Chapter 17: Dealing With A Different Type Of Character From Friendly To Badass . 155

Chapter 18: Additional Questions To Ask And Things To Avoid 170

Chapter 19: Interacting In Group Conversations 177

Conclusion 181

Introduction

There's never a time that we don't talk with others. In some way or the other it is essential to engage with others, whether we've been friends with people for an extended period of time, or if we've just have met them for the first time. The need to talk to others is a necessity since it is essential to creating and strengthening relationships. It is therefore essential to learn how to converse along with the craft of small talking.

This book outlines practical steps and strategies for engaging in discussion in any setting and navigating to build confidence in a group.

You no longer have to fret about the issues that you encounter when talking to someone you've just have met. After reading this book you'll be more confident when dealing with people regardless of whether you know them or not.

The first chapter in this book will discuss why it's important to possess excellent conversations, and why it is essential in order to be able to make small talking. The second chapter offers suggestions on how to maintain an approachable body language. The third chapter focuses on when and how to pose questions and the best questions to ask you keep conversation moving and lively. The fourth chapter focuses on the fact the fact that conversations are one-way communication by providing the tips for how to listen attentively. The fifth chapter provides you with appropriate manners to keep in mind when communicating with your listener, especially if you are talking to them for the first time.

Chapter 1: Conversation As A Skill And Art

Conversation is a casual exchange of ideas or thoughts via speaking.When someone speaks and gets an answer, it's already in the process of forming a conversation.

One does not need to be taught to communicate in a conversation with another people.It is something everyone ought to be doing at some point in their everyday life.However engaging in a conversations is an entirely different issue.

Some people do not have the ability to carry on long and engaging conversations. Some say only those with imagination and charisma are able to be able to hold a conversation the longest time.Some even say that keeping the conversation is like making art.

Conversation can be regarded as an art.Just like compositions and painting Conversations also start with an idea created by an urge or feeling.It could also be a result of desire to share ideas or simply from a desire to have a fun conversation with your acquaintances.

It's an art form because the execution requires more creativity instead of intelligence.People can speak in gibberish however, they can still have an enjoyable conversation, the same way as a professional artist who can paint abstract works could make an amazing work.

As an art form, great conversations are not only about communicating what one wants to communicate.Instead it encourages people to think about it and enjoy it.

It is not necessary to be a naturally charismatic and charismatic person to be able to keep conversations.It is also regarded as a talent that can be learned, taught and improved.

In the end, there are two types of artists: the natural born as well as the systematic artist.If an artist who is systematically trained is eager to learn, he could be able to create masterpieces as well.

Are you a conversationalist or a communicator?

Conversation is a type of communication.A skilled communicator can be a great conversationalist however, not all conversationalists are excellent communicators.

Conversation is frequently referred to as communication because both involve communicating one's thoughts or message to someone else or an audience. Despite the resemblance, conversation differs from communication in a variety of ways.

Conversation is talking, whereas communication is telling. The first stimulates or aims to stimulate a reply from the other person or the audience, while the latter aims to declare one's thoughts. Having a conversation involves both talking and listening. Communication involves only telling what the speaker wants to declare, think or wish to accomplish.

Conversations are spontaneous while communication is considered and thought of. The first comes from an unintentional antecedent, whereas the second is a result of an established topic.

Conversation is used in developing and strengthening social relationship.It is usually made in informal situations.Communication, on the other hand, is used in lecturing or reporting.

Finally, conversation is an art form, while communication is an skill.The one is an art since it relies on imagination, while the second is built on intelligence.If someone learns to communicate effectively and with a sense of humor then he will become an expert in conversation.

Important to have a great conversation

It opens opportunities for new friendships.Strangers can easily become acquainted with just a good conversation.When a person enjoys a conversation with the other parties, he may invite them to another gathering to continue their conversations.These conversations may develop into friendships.

It deepens and strengthens relationships.Relationships may develop from good conversations.A good conversation does not only convey words or ideas, but also shares and touch another person's feelings.It gives a person the opportunity to know the real personality of another.Likewise, it gives the opportunity for the person to share a bit of himself to those he wants to have a deeper relationship with.

It makes the occasion or the party enjoyable.Conversation is essential in a party.It makes the party enjoyable even if it is just a small house party.Most guests prefer to converse more with other party guests than dancing or other party activities.If the host fails to engage in conversations with his guests or fails to make them converse with each other, the party may become boring. People may find excuses for leaving the party early.

A lively conversation might be the most delicious meal the host could serve at the event. It could even make up for other things the party is lacking.

It can boost a business.If the owner has a great conversational skills and has a good rapport with his customers, he will easily earn the confidence of his consumers.The customers may use with his services or purchase the item he's selling because of this trust. Restaurants as well as salons and other companies that engage in guest relations services could gain a lot of benefits when their staff members are skilled conversators.

Chapter 2: The Psychological Benefits Of Small Talk

After we have learned the roots of small talk, and how it's practiced across the globe is the time to shift gears and explore the advantages of engaging in small talk. There are many benefits you can enjoy when you engage in small talks every each day. There have been many studies conducted on the subject of small talks and the positive effects on the physical and mental health. This chapter we'll discuss the advantages of small talks, the ways it affects your ability to speak in public and improve your confidence.

What are the Benefits of Small Talk

Mammals are social creatures and require interaction with other mammals. Take a look at any animal that lives on land or at sea: They're always with their own species as well as other species living in this circle. Being social isn't something we're forced to do It's something that is deeply ingrained in us that is required to be a part of our lives.

Begin to consider the number of small-talk conversations you engage in every day. You get up, dress ready, and go to your local cafe on your route to work. You take a few minutes to chat to the barista. This is a casual conversation. And then you're working in an elevator talking to someone while you sit waiting on the elevator to arrive at your floors. It's just small talk. You go out for lunch and chat with your coworker and the friend who you've never seen and then you have a small chat. The waitress appears and they have more small chatter, and so on. The day isn't even half over and you can see all the activities you've been having.

But this might not be the scenario for all. A lot of people work from home, work for themselves or do not have a reason to talk for hours throughout the day. There are those who could go through a whole day without talking to anyone particularly in the modern age where technology is in our reach. If you're one of them then you could be thinking throughout the day that you're not getting something or there could be an overwhelming feeling of being lonely. This is an active decision you're making and it's something that could be addressed by simply going out the front door and engaging in a little talks everywhere you travel.

Let's look at the primary benefits of small talk that it allows for pleasant interactions with people who you don't have contact with. It's a means to connect with people in our lives, and as such it helps build you up and gives you a sense of belonging. Conversations are the first the beginning of any connection either friendship or relationship. It's the first step.

It is evident that not every conversations can lead to the formation of a lasting friendship. However, consider the people you have bonded with today and for many times, there was a point that these people were not even close to you. However, when you met them--whether at school or at a party or at work, you had a chat and soon began to talk to each other and shared memories with them building stronger bonds. The whole thing is the result of small conversation.

It's been established that small talk can boost your mental wellbeing. If there's a deficiency of it, there's an absence of human connection and this can lead to feelings of loneliness and isolation. In a global population of more than 7 billion individuals, there's no reason to feel lonely. it is really a mental state and a fear of appearing foolish. In the most extreme cases, people spend for a long time without engaging in social activities until it becomes an anxiety to talk with people. Humans are naturally drawn to the sensation of being relaxed and don't want to step away from their own home and prefer to remain safe. What's more relaxing than staying in your home watching TV, not needing to interact with anyone? However, sadness will slowly creep into the room, and the desire for connection with others is stronger than ever.

Small talk can be a important factor, even if you did not realize it. In our modern day and age (something we'll discuss more deeply in a future chapter) it is becoming increasing use of text messages and less and less face-to-face interactions. We all desire it. Are you looking to build deeper connections in your relationships? Are you seeking an ideal partner? The small conversation is where it all begins.

Beyond the mental health aspect Talking with friends can be extremely beneficial professionally. The business world is full of conversation. Many workers aren't their most trusted friends, and so every encounter (outside of business-related conversations) is conversation at its best. This is the minimum amount of exchange of pleasantries to help your through the day. It is usually done in the lunchroom or in an elevator with a person.

If you are apathetic and make little talk, you'll never make a good impression on any person. Don't give up on any chances of being promoted or progressing to the top of an organization. People who advance are the ones who leave lasting impressions. They're the ones who know their boss's kids' names and are always asking the appropriate questions, and are easy to reach. They're the ones that those who the bosses of the business would like to join for the weekend getaway together.

If you're hoping to make more money and reach your goals in career making small talk an absolute requirement. A lot of the time, individuals who climb up the ladder aren't always the most effective in their field however, they're the most pleasant to work with, and also the most friendly to talk to. Talking to people in small talk can go far and can increase your heart and pocket while you're at it.

Another advantage of engaging in small chats is the effect you have on the people around you and the way you are talked about. Did you remember high school, the days when popularity was the only thing was important? It was all about a popularity contest. The older you grow the more likely you are to focus less on being famous and more about being loved. You want every person who interacts with you to be able to spread positive information about who you are as well as your positive impact on others.

Small talk is a method to express your charming personality and create an impression on people. It is important for everyone who speaks to you even for a few minutes in line someplace you meet, to enjoy a positive experience. This could result in people recommending your services or relationships, and shouting your praises for all to be able to hear.

People want to ask, "Have you ever met the person you've mentioned there?" "Yes, she (or she) is amazing. It's a pleasure to meet them." A different thing that small conversations can create in other people is the desire to remain in contact with you in the future. A good small talk is among the most effective methods to make someone want to to know you.

Another advantage of small-talk is that it can help you build wonderful romantic relationships when you use it to the very best of your abilities. Small talk is essential for those who are on the lookout for a new partner. Small talk is at the start of every date with people you do not know, whether you're meeting through the recommendation of a friend, or through the use of an application, or simply going out on a blind date. It all starts by having a small chat: learning about their background, the things they're interested in, and what they do, without being intrusive or too personal. This is the time to make your impression. And by applying the methods you've that you learned in Chapter 1 when you meet someone with whom who you like you can get them to want to meet you next time!

What happens if you work at home? What if there isn't the ability to engage in conversation? In all likelihood, you already have a circle of close family members and friends.

In the end, it all comes down to your being active and going to places that force you to be outside of your home. This is a must particularly for those who desire more social interaction within their daily lives. There are some who have jobs like sales which require a lot of conversation and getting to meet new people every everyday. However, there are also those of us who have been within the same area for many years, but haven't ever met a stranger and hardly made any new connections for many years.

This can be easily changed by going to spaces where people are able to talk. The first thing that can be thought of is in a bar or club where most people visit to talk with others. These establishments are designed to make new acquaintances.

But, they aren't for everyone, me included and I've found the most effective way to meet new people is to join groups that meet regularly to discuss subjects you're interested in. Are you interested by film? There are film clubs in each city where members meet to discuss current films and then watch the films. Are you keen on sports? Find an Fantasy League that meets regularly or join a recreational team. Do you enjoy reading? Join the book club. There's no limit to what you can do in the search for ways to have a conversation If you're struggling to locate anything, then the truth is you're not looking enough!

The benefits of conversation are endless and it's amazing to observe the positive impact small talk can bring into people's lives. You may be able to spot sad people, the ones who carry a sense of sadness in their lives in any setting, be it at work or at a gathering. It is a good time to utilize your new abilities to chat for the benefit of others. Making someone feel appreciated is extremely satisfying to you and it can also create a new friend in the process! Being curious, actively listening, recollecting their names and making eye contact can make them feel valued and appreciated. It's something I always attempt to do whenever I am able to.

How using small Talk can help you become an Improved Public Speaker

Have you ever experienced a nightmare when you're in the midst of a crowd and don't know which words to use? The spotlight is shining on your eye, the sweat runs across your cheeks, you struggle trying to come up with the perfect words. Public speaking is a big worry for many people and if this describes your situation, you're not alone.

There's something extremely frightening that comes with standing in front of a large group of people and giving an address. It can be incredibly frightening and leave you feeling incredibly vulnerable. There are people who will do anything to avoid speaking in public, in order to protect themselves from embarrassment. Did you realize that , the more often you participate in small conversations, the more of public speaking skills you improve your public speaking skills? This may sound to be a bit naive, but it's a fact.

Small talk is a way to ease your nerves when you are talking to other people. Although it is just between you and someone else it helps you prepare to think on your feet and understanding what's good to say and what's not acceptable to say. It helps you engage with that particular person, and it can lead to you as an active public speaker on stage.

The bottom line is that small talk can be a method to improve your skills to speak. If it's public speaking as well as private chats, small talk can give the opportunity to speak confidently. The more you practice and the more comfortable you'll become. If you're facing public speaking tasks coming in the near future, whether at work or wedding etc.--simply consider it a conversational. If you imagine that the crowd isn't as big and think of it as more of an intimate conversation it will make you feel more relaxed. People tend to be drawn to people who are more approachable in public speaking or someone they feel is speaking directly to them.

Some other suggestions for public speaking are also related to small speech. The first tipis to simply be patient. In many types of conversation believe that they have to speed through the conversation or, if they fail to keep the conversation going quickly the person who is talking with them will be bored, and the conversation will be ruined. It's not the situation.

People require time to process new information. You are able to take your time as you're talking. It is possible to think about what you're going to say and then speak it out. This can create more impact, particularly during public speaking. It also lets you say what you have to say.

Another suggestion is smiling. Humans naturally do, and it's the easiest way to incorporate it into conversation or public appearances. Smiles are a great way to fill people's hearts and make them feel comfortable. Everyone doesn't want to listen to people talk in a serious manner for a long time; it causes people to feel uncomfortable. If you're comfortable the audience will also be comfortable.

Start thinking about every conversation as a test run that will lead to future opportunities to speak in public. There is no pressure to engage in small talks. It's simply the conversation between you and a different person (or occasionally, a few more). When you start to feel comfortable in small conversations it will be sure expand over into whatever public presentation that you might need to perform.

Small talk is a method to feel comfortable in your own way without having to worry about what everyone else thinks of you. One of the greatest advantages to public speaking is the fact that you generally have notes with you, so often you do not have to think in a hurry. Notes can serve as a safeguard which guides you in the direction you want to talk, easing any pressure you may be feeling.

In small talk as well as public speaking, to feel comfortable, you must increase your confidence. Let's take a look at how confidence can play a role in small talk, and the relationship between them.

How using small Talk Will Make You Feel More confident

Have presented with a talk about confidence? "Be assured" and "get your confidence back" are words that most of us have all our lives. This is due to the fact that confidence is an essential factor in all fields and in all activities. From arts and sports to from teaching to business having a lot of confidence is crucial to getting your life's objectives.

How does conversational can be incorporated in this? Now is how do you assess your confidence in approaching someone new to chat? Do you make the effort without hesitation? Do you occasionally opt not to because of fear? In the majority of cases, it's the former. Conversation with strangers is not an easy task. It's stressful to be in the unknown, interacting with people you might not have any commonality with.

Sometimes, our mind plays tricks on us, and we imagine an event in which the worst can happen. We do the wrong thing and end up causing anger to the person and then get humiliated in front of the entire world with the greatest humiliation that could be imaginable however, how could it occur? We believe these things to fool ourselves into staying away from conversation altogether. We might say that we lack enough confidence to engage in small-talk. But what if I informed you that engaging in small talk can actually boost your confidence each time you engage in it?

Sometimes it is necessary to be bold in your conversation. You might be negotiating an uninitiated date in the very first instance, and truly hope that this one is successful. There could be an opportunity to speak to the person who is responsible for the next promotion in your business. The stakes are quite high. If you don't engage in conversation These scenarios are likely to be very difficult to get into right immediately. Your confidence might be low and nerves are capable of playing games using our bodies and our minds. Your hands sweat and your heart beats faster as you begin to stutter and it could be a problem. This is the reason why the more you speak in small groups more comfortable it becomes similar to riding on a bicycle.

Consider the situation this way: Each time you make conversation you're adding more layers to the foundation that you're building your self-confidence. Every time you try it, it improves and you're more at ease because you've been through this before. In time, it will become similar to muscle memory. If you gain the confidence to be confident enough, that will flow into other areas in your daily life. You'll be able to ask for an extra hour off or asking your girlfriend to take you out for dinner since you've conquered one of the biggest anxieties that plague our society at present. You'll be able to speak and rise to the top professionally and socially. Are you aware of all the advantages we mentioned earlier? So, add some the confidence of that group.

Small talk can be described as being vulnerable. It's a risk to be vulnerable with a stranger. Imagine the level of confidence that you'll feel when you don't have to think about it. There isn't anyone that is intimidating enough to prevent you from walking up and greeting them. Your head will be held up high with your shoulders back, a big smile, radiating confidence. This is someone I'd like to meet and that is someone I would like to hire and that is someone I would like to talk to on a casual basis.

Chapter 3: Strategies For Small Talk Conversations

Here's a character Richard Nixon, who was not a fan of small talk, was not a fan to meet strangers and was awkward physically, and then he enters the only business which requires ease with strangers, and a talent for small conversation.

Harry Shearer Harry Shearer

Following the guidelines that are provided in this chapter, conversers can enhance their conversation skills, engage in more meaningful conversations, and improve their social likability.

Ask questions about the other Person

Studies show that by being interested in people and offering them the chance to talk about themselves, it is possible to generate positive feelings within other people. For instance, in an investigation conducted in 2012 conducted by Diana I. Tamir and Jason P. Mitchell titled sharing information about oneself is intrinsically rewarding. Sharing details about oneself is associated with an increase in activity in the part of the brain which is linked to enjoyment. Indeed, some individuals were willing to pay for this chance. The truth is, sharing personal information can cause individuals to feel better. So, you can create a positive atmosphere for others by arranging your small-talking conversations to offer the opportunity for your conversation partner to talk about him or herself. This can be done by being interested in their lives and asking them questions.

Inquiring questions shows curiosity and gives others the chance to talk about themselves. For instance, an office worker may ask his new coworker, "Why did you apply to this job?" This question gives the coworker a chance to talk about her personal details like her professional goals, aspirations and working philosophies.

When the first date, a person may inquire of their partner, "How long have you been in this region?" This question opens an opportunity for sharing of information , such as your previous experiences in the region as well as fun activities locally.

In the classroom, students may ask a classmate something such as, "Why did you choose this particular class?" This question invites the student to share details such as their educational goals, specialization, as well as their previous experiences at the school or professors they have had.

Of course office work or a first date and the scenarios in the classroom above offer only three instances of infinite questions one could pose about someone else. People who are in the real world must ask open-ended, open-ended questions that relate to their current situation and require disclosure of their personal information. If you happen to find yourself with some time to spare, think of coming up with three questions you can ask someone in your environment.

Sharing personal information is satisfying. It's true that people dedicate 60 percent of their time self-talk according to R.I. Dunbar, A. Marriott, and N.D. Duncan's 1997 studyon the Human Conversational Behavior. If you are able to make your partner feel relaxed when they talk to you it is likely that they will be impressed and will want to speak to you again in the near future.

Contact us for follow-up questions.

Answering open-ended questions that are less abstract encourages more sharing, and will give you and your conversation partner something tangible to talk about. You can try relating the question to the initial question and then provide an answer. For instance, if the office worker asks his new colleague "Why did you decide to apply to this job?", the new colleague could answer by saying something similar to "I was looking to move nearer to my family, and I am very impressed by the company's green policy."

With this response that office worker has a number of pieces of information to create a conversation from. The coworker who was new admitted that he used travel farther than he is currently, lives near to his office and that he is concerned about the environmental conditions. In this instance, the most advanced employee can choose one of these topics that interests him , and ask a follow-up question on the topic. For instance, he could ask "How long was your previous journey?" By doing this the more experienced employee shows his interest which encourages sharing and can open the door to the possibility of introducing many more topics for discussion. If you're watching the talk shows, be sure to pay close attention to the guest's response to host's questions. Find an appropriate follow-up question to pose to the host in a more restricted time.

You can share information about yourself

Like getting others to share information, sharing information about yourself can be beneficial. The science further discusses the benefits of sharing personal information. Nancy L. Collins and Lynn Carol Miller reveal in their study from 1994 Self-Disclosure and Liking The Meta-Analytic Review, that disclosure of self is as an essential part of long-term relationships. The study revealed that sharing information about self increases the likability of people and leads others to reveal themselves and open up in return.

In the beginning, researchers discovered that sharing personal information increases the likelihood of being liked by others. That is the more details one provides about themselves is the more share a similarity to themselves. However people who do not share as much information about themselves be less likable. The refusal to reveal details about yourself implies that the person is concealing something or keeping a secret.

The second reason is that doing self-disclosure could encourage your friend to reveal details regarding themselves. Collins and Miller discovered that people are more likely to divulge the most information to people they enjoy the most. Keep in mind that sharing personal information increases one's popularity. If you are more likable increases the chance that others will share information with you information about yourself. This will bring out the positive feeling you would like your conversations to create for yourself and your friends.

In the context of an office employee and a new coworker discussing their commutes, let's look at the way in which an opportunity for the senior employee to reveal their personal information is manifested within the dialogue. The employee and coworker's conversation may be like this:

Office Staff: "Hi! We've not had the opportunity to speak much and I was just curious about what inspired you to apply to this job?"

New coworker: "Well, the commute is much easier than what my previous job was. Also, I'm a major admirer of the company's green policy."

Office worker: "I see. How far did you commute for your last job?"

New coworker: "About ninety minutes each way."

(Here the most experienced employee is able to talk about his experiences the commute.)

Office employee: "That's wild. I used to work in the music industry which was basically the exact each weekend. I would drive to a certain city, sometimes just a few hours away, and do my job, then drive for hours back home the following day.

What was the longest commute you've ever taken?"

Through sharing information with one others, the two participants were able to connect to each other's experiences regarding commutes. In this instance, the conversers must be aware of their conversation partner's body language for clues to how to proceed with the conversation.

Be aware of body language

Body language can reveal a significant amount of people's moods, attitudes, feelings and thoughts. Certain forms of body language encourage conversations while others signal the desire to be alone. Research conducted by at the University of California, Los Angeles claim that more than 50% of human communication takes place via body language. By paying close attention to and understanding the signals that come from people's body language conversers can utilize this information to react appropriately.

The feet of other people can provide the most important clues regarding their interest in conversation. The reports from the FBI indicate that people tend to keep at individuals and things they don't want to engage with. That is people tend to point their feet at those things they love most. So, if people pointing their feet toward your when you are in the area, take it as an opportunity to start a conversation with them. However If someone shifts his or her foot away from you, take that signal to take them off your feet.

In determining whether someone else is interested and is eager to continue conversations, make sure you pay careful pay attention to their body language to your own. People are inclined to imitate the body language of the people whom they're open to. If you sit back on your chair and your companion is doing the same thing and vice versa, consider it an indication that they that they can carry the conversation. If people are bonded to each other, they tend to adopt the same postures, gestures and postures.

Additionally, a genuine smile shows an interest. To determine if a smile is genuine take a look at the person's eyes, not their mouth. If someone truly smiles and is genuine, the outer edges of their eyes may be wrinkled. Dermatologists describe permanent wrinkles in the eye area as "crow's feet. Check for tiny folds on the skin around the temples which run outwards from the outside of the eye towards their ears. Eye wrinkles are not evident in fake smiles.

However, the body language could indicate that they are not ready to continue an exchange. If this is the case, you should respect their body language and acknowledge that they're not ready to engage in conversation. Most likely they have something else to be thinking about which take precedence over the desire to talk Don't ignore these signals. Disinterested signals that are non-verbal include a jaw that is tightly closed with raised eyebrows or bent arms, folded legs, and an extended nod at the top of your head.

The first sign of a tightened jaw is a sign that the individual is feeling stressed. Stress can manifest due to a variety of reasons. The stress levels of people are usually outside your control. If someone appears to be stressed, give them some space and then continue the conversation at an suitable moment. A tightened neck and a wrinkled-up brow are typical of the stressor's jaw clenched.

If someone's eyes are in a raised position, they may be feeling various types of unpleasant emotions, like worry or fear. Naturally, if your conversation is about information that could trigger anxiety or fear like a possible hurricane, it is likely that your partner's expressions of body language will indicate anxiety (at at least, you ought to hope that it does!) But if the topic of conversation doesn't suggest worry the conversation partner's eyebrows could suggest that the conversation is likely to be over soon.

If someone raises his arms they demonstrate the inability to accept conversations partner's opinions. It is possible to have a conversation with a nice person however, folded arms indicate that they do not want to in having a conversations. The arms that are folded up create an physical barrier that indicates an intellectual reticence to the ideas of another. Legs that are folded indicate an identical attitude. If you observe during a small conversation that the person is sitting with their legs or arms crossed for a long duration, don't believe that they aren't interested in meeting you. They might have something else in their minds, and thus are resisting your input in conversation in order to concentrate on something else more important.

Then, a prolonged head nod signifies a deep desire to be admired. If someone nods frequently while they listen to your voice, it suggests that they want to be impressed with them. In this way, they is more interested in getting your approval rather than going the conversation in a casual manner. In this instance, you can offer an acknowledgement of an aspect they have told you about them. A compliment can provide them with the confidence they seek. Once they have been validated, they are able to shift their attention to the message of the conversation, and away from the need to prove themselves.

The body language of a person can indicate the extent to which a person is willing to engage in conversation. If you happen to examine a photograph of someone, take note of the way they move. Try to guess how they'd be willing to engage in conversation with someone new.

If body language that is negative displays its presence during conversation people can respond to the signals with courtesy stopping the conversation.

Succeeding in Small Talk

Small talk conversations are over. People who are engaged in small talk or move on to other matters of greater significance or end their conversations entirely. This section offers guidelines to end small conversation in a positive manner. If you decide it's appropriate to cut the conversation short, you should make an honest, positive comment and follow it up with an overview on the discussion or a rationale to end the conversation.

A sincere positive comment ends small-talk conversations. In the majority of situations an expression such as "nice meeting you" is enough. Your comment could be to be focused on a specific aspect of the conversation. For instance when discussing the latest project with your colleague you could say something to the like "I'm glad we got to chat. The conversation has given me many ideas for our next project." Following an initial date, one partner may announce the end of their interaction by saying, "I had so much pleasure the evening. The show was incredible." Such statements make it appear as if the conversation is coming to an end. In the present, try to reflect on the most recent conversation you had. think of one good idea you can share about the conversation.

After making a sincere, positive comment, write down the exchange. As an example, imagine you've had a brief conversations with a classmate on the hallway of your school. For the end of the conversation with a genuine positive, encouraging comment, like "I enjoyed having a conversation with you" and then provide a concise outline of the benefits from the conversation, such as "I'm grateful to know that I'm not the only person who feels this feeling about Professor Walt's class." A summary let people know that you learned something from the exchange and that you have absorbed the information they shared, and wishes to continue the conversation. Now, try to recall the last conversation you had and then summarize it in just one or two phrases.

In addition conversers can choose to follow their notes by preparing plans for the future. This can take various forms, such as the invitation to have a subsequent conversation, actions that either or both parties could undertake after they have parted ways and the vague possibility of meeting again.

In the beginning, they can invite one another to meet with each other again. The office colleagues could conclude by arranging to talk with each other during the next meeting. A simple statement such as "I will meet you at the next meeting" is a good illustration of a plan. For a casual setting the new acquaintances could make a statement like "I'm going to visit the skate park that's new on the third of tomorrow at 3:00, If you'd like to join my there." In all cases the plan must be a signal that one person in the conversation wants to keep in touch with each other. If someone ends the conversation with a suggestion to meet again, make it as an invitation to meet with them for a second time.

In addition, plans are formulated as an action that is to be planned for the future. For instance, you may tell your friend following an argument regarding movies, "I will check out the alien film you mentioned to me." The future action suggests a desire to talk to someone else. In this case both of you will likely discuss the movie that you saw the next time you meet them.

Thirdly, the vagueness regarding future interaction are a different kind of strategy. For instance for a conversations with a comment such as "See you later!" or "I'll catch you up later." Make vague words like these when you'd be content to see another person and you'd be comfortable not coming in contact for a time.

Or, a reason to stop the conversation may be followed by a sincere , positive statement. When you provide the person on the other side of your conversation a reason to leave and politely conclude the exchange. The reasons for leaving indicate that the conversants do not desire to end their conversation, but rather they have other matters to address. If a student is making small talk with a classmate could make a note with a rationale for leaving , and then formulate an ending statement to the conversation, such as "It's been great talking to you. However, I must go to the library to finish my task." This student provides his classmate a reason to stop the conversation. The student's classmates have the option to propose an idea to the future, or not.

For a way to conclude a casual conversation, suggest that you'd like to conclude the conversation by making a positive comment. After that, provide an overview, a overview with a plan give a reason to leave. Find an explanation for why you should leave your current job which you can share with another person.

Chapter 4: What Is Small Talk Important?

We have previously discussed the reasons we engage in small-talk however, what makes small talk so crucial?

You don't know where it's going to lead you.

The small talk option is no-cost alternative. It is possible to engage in small conversations with anyone and pay nothing to do it. There's no risk to you. They either like you or dislike you, both of them are to your favor. Being loved by strangers is great for your ego, and being snubbed by strangers has no significance in your life. It is impossible to think about where a few minutes of slack-minded chatter could bring you to an acquaintance, new informational source or even get a beneficial outcome when it comes to business relationships.

It makes you smarter

According to a study recently conducted by researchers from the University of Michigan, our mental capacity to deal with many issues is enhanced when we interact with others socially. If you meet any person, especially in the beginning, try to figure out that the person in front of you admires or curious about the things you say. The process churns the gears inside your brain, enhancing your deductive skills and helping you gain perspective in your life. As your skills in deductive reasoning improve with time, it becomes simpler to work on problems, like solving the Sudoku puzzle or crossword, which requires you to think things through.

You're feeling good about yourself.

A lot of us, particularly the introverts, the idea of engaging in social interactions with others can be exhausting. Do you find yourself constantly talking to people that you don't even have a relationship with? Absolutely terrifying! However, take awhile and reflect how many times having a conversation with someone lightheartedly has made you feel more relaxed? What number of times simply discussing something that isn't serious or even about things that are fun can make you feel a lot better? Like we said, human beings are social creatures. Whatever you might dislike talking to strangers or be anxious but deep inside you feel more relaxed and comfortable. This is the way we are wired and, while whether we like to or not, but it is a fact that we always feel more relaxed after a conversation, even if it's the occasional chatter between an individual you'll never meet again.

Enhances your concentration

When you engage in conversations with someone else, you're obliged to pay attention to the person you are talking to said even if you're trying to be polite and don't care the things they say. This can increase your attention span since you have to listen attentively to what they have to say, in order you don't offend their. This is also a way to remove your eyes from your phone and force you to be aware of the surroundings around you, which that you might not have previously done in normal situations.

People will love you

It's a straightforward formulafor making friends - you must have people who be like you. It is a rule of thumb that people will not befriend people they don't like. (Would you be interested in a friendship with one who is like a snob?) To be liked , you must to be viewed as personable. People appreciate people who are able to engage in conversations and who have engaging ways of communicating with them. However, this doesn't mean people who aren't confident or who have difficulty holding conversations aren't able to make friends. All you have to do is build confident and make that first move. Small talk isn't just about being attractive or having fun and engaging stories to tell. Small conversations show respect for the person you're talking to. They will feel appreciated to you taking the time to speak to them, and they ultimately, they'll like them. This can help you make many acquaintances and business connections quickly.

That's the way things work.

There is no option to remain uninvolved. In this modern world, small talk is vital to gain an employment, to work effortlessly with colleagues, create new clients, and to ensure your existing clients are satisfied - you cannot be content with it. To be successful in your career, you must be able to communicate about, engage and impress those who are important to you or the other person to you. It is impossible to back away from saying"this isn't my coffee". Conversations, no matter how smallcrucial for making that crucial leap forward in life. If you're not able to think for yourself businesses will be cautious about hiring you, regardless of whether you have attended the Ivy League school and graduated within one of the highest 10% in your class. In the present, it's not the knowledge you have that counts, but the ability to put your ideas into words. You have to be able sell yourself through your words. Long lengthy conversations aren't going to cut it the trick, as time is of the essence and people like people who are concise and still be impressive.

Chapter 5: The Potential And Importance Of Small Talks

Small talk is a crucial method of communication. It is not necessary to discuss complex topics. The most trivial topics will suffice (ex. the weather, the food at a restaurant, the traffic, music and so on.). It's important since it allows you to make connections with people in an effective manner. It is possible to think it's not necessary however it's extremely important. It is actually conversational, and it helps to maintain your bond connections, contact and bond with your colleagues, friends and business partners.

Refining and reworking the things you must say in small conversations will make you realize how valuable and efficient it can be. It is not only in building excellent relationships, but also to expand and extend your network. If you approach it in a positive manner in conjunction with well-organized body language, you'll be able to manage your day-to-day life and concentrate more on the achievement.

To make new acquaintances it is important to build a foundation of good communication and shared interests. This can be achieved through small conversations. They allow you to gain space which allows you to see the potential in all kinds of communication. Additionally, it gives you the possibility of declining or agree to an engagement.

In the course of establishing small discussions it is vital to know the three essential phases of communication.

Small talk stage will help you create a positive mood for the person you are planning to talk to. At this point you must make sure that you are exact when communicating with the person you are talking to. In this instance it is essential to utilize the correct manner of speaking and your body. Your aim is to engage your conversational partner making him desire to move on to the next stage.

Professional conversation - After you have passed the small talk stage you are now able to move on to the next phase of conversation or communication, that is more professional in its nature. This involves discussing typical topics for reference. This is also the time when you use professional terminology.

Many people are more relaxed in this stage. It's when they can find something they share with the people they're speaking to which makes them want to continue to have authentic and profound conversations with substance.

A personal and intimate conversation This is the most intense phase in the process of communication. In this phase when you speak to an individual as if it were an intimate colleague, family member or acquaintance. In this scenario you can safely believe that the conversation has grown more intimate, personal and passionate.

Here are some of the positive aspects that you can enjoy when you decide to become an expert in small-sized talks. Knowing these advantages will allow you to consider small talk not just as unimportant, but instead as crucial elements of your day-to-day life.

This leads to better and bigger opportunities

The thing that makes these small conversations so crucial and effective is that they could lead to greater and better opportunities, each of which is beneficial for both your professional and personal development. It's the best way to understand your fellow colleagues. It is the most important factor to making new friends connecting with them, and learning more about the things you have in common and also your individual differences.

People may see conversations that are small as being trivial however, they are crucial to understanding the people in your life. They help you build more intimate friendships, relationships and connections. Being able to communicate with anyone about anything allows you to be open to a variety of possibilities and connections.

But, there's one obstacle that can hinder engaging in small conversations - and that's anxiety. particularly when you're an introvert who is shy, or are just an individual who is uncomfortable in a social environment. But, if you allow your anxiety to rule you, then you'll miss out on a lot of opportunities. You're missing out on opportunities to meet someone with the same interests as you do and is competent to provide you with details about the field you're in, or about your interests.

Simply put small talk can be useful in determining how you're linked to the people who are around you. By doing this, you'll be aware of your shared intentions and aspirations. These connections serve as a few opportunities to make your lives more enjoyable.

It helps you leave a positive impression

Small talk provides you with an opportunity to impart your knowledge with the people you're talking to. You can read their mood - which means that you can learn about the way people view your expertise and how they perceive you. By using conversation, you are able to quickly explore the human landscape.

It allows you to impress people with how it permits you to try different things. One example is the jokes of the people who are around you, their possible sensitivities , and also other details about their personalities. It is also possible to leave your impression with a positive impression, without making a big mistake.

Build lasting friendships

Imagine your most intimate acquaintances and colleagues. What is the way you began your relationship? Didn't it start with small conversations? Small conversations are the foundation of many connections and friendships. Talking with someone for only one or two minutes can allow you to make a lasting acquaintance. Many married couples begin by having small conversations and it's safe to claim that this could be the way to meet the perfect partner for life.

Breaks the silence

Small talk is also an icebreaker, particularly when you're meeting people for the first time. The benefit of this is that it increases your confidence. It usually requires an enormous amount of confidence to even begin small discussions. For greater confidence, you should be relaxed and concentrate on being you. Do not try too hard or altering yourself to be a part of the crowd. This is only going to cause you to stress yourself out excessively and could result in a negative outcome, particularly if people close to you are noticing that you're anxious and nervous.

Talking to small groups should be about breaking up the silence with a more natural way. When you are preparing yourself to talk to someone who you do not know, bear in mind that the person you are talking to is most likely to be at lost for words too. The art of talking to people even over minor issues doesn't require you to know the exact words that you need to communicate in all situations. In the majority of cases it's simply about being polite by speaking up.

To manage your anxieties and fears to manage your anxiety and nervousness, you must be honest. It is also recommended to acknowledge the circumstances. In the case of, for example, if you are in a position in which you have to interact with many people and you are in a situation where there is a lot of noise, the best way to deal with it is to feel at ease, then stop the silence. The best part about the latter is it can make everyone feel more relaxed and at relaxed. Talk about something that anyone can relate to. This is the primary factor in starting small discussions.

If you've been able to manage this scenario and break the silence with ease and successfully, you'll be able to increase your confidence. You'll feel more confident every time you are able to manage the small talk you've attempted. In time, you'll be able to get it down and be amazed by how confident you've gotten when speaking to people.

It inspires new ideas

Chatting with a friend or even a stranger can be an excellent way to get inspired and generate new ideas. You can generate fresh thoughts and ideas through this. When you talk to someone you feel uncomfortable with initially it is possible to think of different ways to approach them.

You'll likely find yourself saying intriguing and unpredictably things in a flash. This is an excellent opportunity to show off your creative side.

Make sure you pay attention

The modern world is populated with people who be more focused on their phones and gadgets instead of connecting with people in their surroundings. Although technological advancements allow us to have access to an abundance of information in a matter of seconds but they also prevent us from creating connections that are real and focusing on what is really important.

When you are buried in the screens of your devices There is a possibility that you'll fail to be present and take in the world that are happening around you. In small, brief chats and a few messages, you'll have to unplug your gadgets for a time and engage with people to break the monotony. You can truly listen, observe and converse with people. It's a great way to remove yourself from the world of technology even for an hour and speak to someone in person.

Apart from the benefits listed above, a few researchers at the University of Michigan also discovered that even small conversations and interactions with friends actually have a positive effects in your capacity to tackle issues. You can expect your problem-solving abilities to improve if you take on the role of someone else often. Be aware of people, engage with them, and truly listen to their thoughts. This is a good method to increase not only your social abilities but also the confidence you have and your ability to resolve issues.

Chapter 6: Talking To Anyone And Feeling At Home

After you've developed an excellent collection of interpersonal skills you will be comfortable engaging with anyone, and that is not just strangers and friends. You may have realized that confidence in yourself is the most important thing you need to make this happen. Being comfortable around other people and feeling relaxed in interacting with others all are a result of being confident about oneself. In the end, how do you feel comfortable with other people if you're not confident in being you?

People who are confident and have high levels of confidence in themselves are those who feel confident about themselves. It is important to note that being confident doesn't be a sign that you think extremely positively about yourself, but simply that you are confident of yourself, of your work and that you're not embarrassed to display those aspects of yourself to people around you.

If you'd like to be able to speak to anyone , and feel confident about it first, start by letting yourself relax. Beware of feeling stressed or anxious by what could take place and what people may think of your character. Instead, relax and allow your mind to wander towards more positive thoughts, rather than worries. Be aware that the thoughts you make and how you feel will be interpreted by those in your vicinity as well.

In opening your mind and your awareness to the positive aspects of your surroundings In addition, you gain the impression of being friendly. People will notice that you aren't too conscious, and this allows them to be open to you on their own. Being able to converse with others does not require you to be the first to initiate the conversation. Rather you must be willing to engage in conversations to ensure that you have a positive interactions with people who are around you.

Another way to feel relaxed speaking with people is to put your attention on them and not on yourself. The people who are excellent at facilitating conversations are able to easily engage in lengthy conversations while not talking at all, by allowing the other person to talk and open up more. When they do this they appear truly thoughtful, and at the same time, they'll are less stressed because they don't have a lot to speak about.

Be aware that conversations should be one of back-and-forth communications or a game of give and take. the ideal scenario is for participants to have the same amount of time discussing and listening. Remember this and make sure you are focusing on the person you're speaking to. Talk to them about their lives, like what they did in the day as well as what the thought about the program you saw, but be sure to think about what you make a question.

In general, the kinds of questions you're permitted to ask will depend on the relationship you have with the person you're speaking to. The relationship should dictate the tone of voice you use and your choice of words. Although turning your attention to the person in question is a great method to show them that you're truly looking forward to a conversation but it could be an offender in the event that you ask the incorrect questions. A single wrong question could turn a pleasant conversation into a awkward situation.

Chapter 7: The Best Ways To Engage Women We Do Not Know

Dear Gentlemen The time is now to provide you with priceless tips on how to become acquainted with women without having to be snubbed due to insufficient behaviour. Before we get started, you'll need to be aware to understand how women's minds work. I guarantee it will save you a lot of hassle and wasted effort. There is a reason why is said that women are from Venus and men come from Mars. Women's psychology is a mystery to ways. Some men believe that they are crazy and irrational, but what do you confront a natural force? You just have to accept it, and you'll get through it.

The first thing you need to be aware of when talking to stranger ladies is they are not a fan of the arrogance of their behaviour. For example, saying "Hey you, sweetheart, is it is this your space is mine or ours?" will get you closer to the doormat. We think that deciding on where it is that you and your partner share as a final decision. But you need to get through every defense she has. When you are trying to meet women, show respect and you're a gentleman. Women are very satisfied with this.

A good manner of conduct coupled with a decent look is also a than a winning combination. It is not necessary to wear an elegant tuxedo. However, you should dress smartly and well-groomed (take an examination at yourself in the mirror prior to you leave and combs aren't an instrument that could cause harm, it's completely safe to utilize) and courteous (good manners are not something you read in a science-fiction book, but rather the gateway to a successful first meeting).

Another thing to keep in mind is that women love to receive compliments. One of my friends once said that men are drawn to their eyes (they want to see stunning legs walking past) while women are more interested in their ears. If you decide to approach her ensure you've got something attractive and beautiful to say, such as "I am amazed by your exquisite hairstyle, it makes you stand out from other people" and "You have a wonderful taste for jewels, and what a amazing bracelet you're wearing". If you're in a more casual situation you could simply offer an appreciation for her hairstyle or how elegantly casual she's dressed. Be sure not to make the wrong compliment, as you'll be exiled from the game of flirting. For instance, if you tell someone that "Although you're not too fat, white looks gorgeous on you" and you get the flashing red light at the same time.

The second thing to do is to always be honest. If you find yourself in private matters like being in contact with someone be honest. The truth will be revealed eventually and the earlier you do it, the more favorable. Let her decide if she wants to remain in love with you or not. It doesn't regardless of whether you're married or not. False statements will not get you anywhere. Women also have invisible lie detectors and they will catch you fast. There is no reason to lose your chance to enjoy an evening of pleasure.

The most important characteristic of a man who draws women is his ability to listen. It is not necessary to comprehend every word she says as long as you are able to respond with a positive attitude. When she's explaining her work-related issues or about how she got into a dispute with a coworker due to the fact that they were both in the same attire at the previous event, show that you're keen to hear what she is saying. Be compassionate and understanding. It will be greatly loved by women.

Another aspect to consider that is difficult if done correctly is to make your friends look appear like you. In most cases women go out in groups. Therefore, be courteous to her companions, but don't give them more attention than you pay to her. Be courteous, give drinks, but don't make her feel like the center of the night. This means you kill two rabbits in one shot She will appreciate you more, and her friends will inspire her to behave more generously towards you. For example, going out for another date.

Don't be too revealing about your own life. First of all , women are just like cats, fascinated to the level of desperation. They love it when a man is lost with mystery. So try to keep the same.

Another thing to remember is that if your focus is solely on yourself, she'll think you are self-centered and selfish who isn't interested in getting to get to know her.

In the end, it is possible to affirm that there are two phrases that will completely make you lose your relationship with women. The first is "I am very boring isn't it?". Women are fairly straightforward and you'll probably receive a yes when you are really focusing on a particular topic. What then? Instead of showing weakness, simply shift the topic when you begin to feel like you're getting boring.

The other is "I don't intend or do not plan on having an intimate relationship.". This is a little snarky and unnatural. Who knows what your relationship's future could become? The first time you meet someone is the only way to know. drink. It is unclear how many you'll need before you know when this experience will end.

In short, be courteous, use good words, and don't do anything that is untrue. Simple as that. Women aren't scientific breakthrough, they are rather a whole universe that has to be discovered.

How to Approach Men We Do Not Know

Ladies, it's your turn to pay attention. The first thing you need to do is be aware that men aren't as straightforward as you believe. They simply use this type of behavior as a suitable cover-up, as they are believed to be more vulnerable than women are. Therefore, there are a few strategies that work each time you're trying to begin a conversation with a male.

In the beginning, you must be aware that men love attractive women. It doesn't matter if you're an ultra slim model. As long as you emit positivity and have a refined look and elegant, you stand a great chance of getting his notice. Don't believe that men don't know anything about fashion, or at the very least, how women should dress and look. Therefore, pick your own style and stick with it. Men will be impressed.

Men are the strongest sexually. Remember that even if you're an independent and strong female, men do not like being dominated. Therefore, be wise and polite. There are numerous methods to make things happen your way , as long as you convince the person that it's his idea.

If you are approached by someone you don't know Don't begin by talking about your current job or top executive position in the company. It is a good time to share these kinds of details. Let him be aware of who you are as a person, to make him feel confident in your professional image. In the event that he doesn't, he could think you're an Amazon woman and that you are the victim. You'd rather not be like him, wouldn't you?

Another thing to be wary of is drinking excessively while you are with people you've just have met. Alcohol is a bad genie, and it can make you look embarrassed. You don't want him consider you to be an alcohol addict. People believe that women who drink are unable to control. He's not going to think about a second date if you prove that your bottle is your most trusted companion.

The way men think is that the next best thing women can do (after buying) is to speak about themselves. Therefore, surprise him by asking him questions about his past. This will help you stand out from other women and make him feel that you're "something other than the rest". Engage him in your work, and you'll make him feel special and unique. Men love this because they're like puppies but they are bigger.

Avoid using bad words, and don't show arrogance. Men have plenty of male buddies to do that. If you demonstrate that you are able to be one of the guys so that you can cut the distance between pair of them, you'll be as you are.

Women love sports as do men. Naturally, you can't be required to know what the outlook is for this season's baseball, but you can always tell something like "I am aware that this team is among the top and have scored a lot of points, but could you give me more details about their top player". The person in question is aware that you're not a fan of baseball, but he'll appreciate or certain that you put in an effort to hear about the passion he has for sports.

When men speak about women, you must prove that you are worthy confidence in yourself to appreciate the attractiveness of other women too. Don't be a snarl when you hear someone comment regarding this issue, just smile and shift the subject to another. Men are friendly and are able to keep their minds busy when you discuss something they are interested in, and not just women. This includes sports, cars fishing, etc.

Don't be a snarky about your previous girlfriend. If he asks if you're seeing someone, respond with a an easy "No" If you are in fact dating. If you begin whining and crying, he'll believe that you're an angry, rejected woman who is unhappy with males. You don't want to be blamed for past mistakes, wouldn't you? There is no need to be the one to pay for someone else's mistakes, so try to keep that negative memory from your own eyes.

Give him a smile and a gentle handshake. The first method is always effective particularly when the conversation gets a bit longer than it is. Smiles show that you love the person you're talking to and is not afraid to express that you love him. Therefore, if you are able to be closer to the mysterious smile that is Mona Lisa, any man would like to know the secrets of your soul.

A casual touch can be a way which shows you are interested. Be gentle, but be subtle in your manner, and you'll be sending the correct message. A gentle touch to the shoulder or hand can be a sign that you truly like the person. Are we required to mention the wonderful sensations of shivers he'll experience?

In the end, here are two phrases that are sure to cause the man you are interested in dial 911 and request backup, or at the very least search to the exit for the fire. The first is "I never ever do this" for instance, when you offer your number to a friend or allow him to kiss you in the middle of the night. The first thing to remember is that nobody believes it, but of obviously you did but you aren't comfortable to admit it, since it's likely not going to be okay at the end. There's no way to ask whether you've ever given your number to a guy following that first encounter. This isn't a problem. In the end, there must be a method to communicate in the near future. Smoke signals have gone out of fashion. The man will believe you're underestimating him and you will believe that falsehood. Therefore, from a purely moral perspective this is not a good phrase to use.

The other rule to avoid should be "What is your opinion about weddings?". If it isn't a clear subject you're talking about, don't mention it. It's as if you give him a shower that is cold and in within a few minutes, you'll be contemplating a few options to escape the situation. He will conclude that you're just a girl trying to tie the rope around his neck. However, it could be that he thinks you're feeling unsecure and that is not an option when you are trying to impress him.

In essence, dress to succeed smile, be enthusiastic, and show an interest in his interests and lifestyle, but don't demonstrate that you are able to take on the world all by yourself and, by touching him lightly provide him with an idea of what you would do when you go out on another date.

How To Get the attention of the public and blow It away

The most talented speakers are frightened when they present themselves to crowds of people and make a speech. The reason behind this is not because they don't know what they should say or are uneasy, but rather since they aren't familiar with who is who are within the space. Everyone is unique and certain individuals prefer to make the speaker uncomfortable. This is why there are times when a speaker may be anxious when he is about to go on stage to speak.

However, on the other hand this is a sign that folks came to hear your words is a sign of respect. They haven't been dragged to the ground, therefore they're expecting to hear from you information that they believe is useful.

Chapter 8: Being Open

There is a chance that you're not an overly self-conscious person There could be a chance that instead of feeling self-conscious you're more a closed-minded person or view the world in a single rigid way.Especially when you're in your senior years, you could find yourself reluctantly stuck on your ways.This section will discuss how to be open to discussion in conversation when the person with whom you're talking has an opposing opinion that is not your own.Even even if you are aware that you are able to disagree with someone's views, the first time you meet someone new, it's recommended to try as hard as you can not do that.This can only cause tension and, if you do meet that person in the future, it is likely to create a negative precedent in the future.

Understanding Your Personal Limitations

If you're thinking of the possibility of opening yourself to new perspectives you're likely to meet during small-talk, it's crucial to be aware of where your own limits lie.Obviously small talk tactics are not a way to encourage discussion on politics in any in any way, but often the person that is part of the conversation might make a political or controversial statement nonetheless.If you're an older person or is angry often, or who has a generally strongly held opinion, it is important to recognize this in yourself.Often after you have identified an individual characteristic about yourself, you'll be recognize the characteristic and refrain from making it clear in a casual conversation.If you're unable to see your own limitations in the realm of conversation and communication, you'll be unable to overcome your weaknesses and grow.

Be cautious when re-enacting the Snap Decision

Another way to show the person whom you're communicating open to many perspectives and perspectives can be to hold your judgments to yourself.While we all are able of filtering our thinking, there are individuals who refuse to let their thoughts go through any kind of filter.There are positive and negative sides to being a person with this trait.A benefit of being this kind of person is that you're typically referred to as having an enthralling and opinionated character; however it is not always the case that this will coincide with the idea of participating in small talk.Even when something comes to mind about an issue it is crucial to take a moment to examine whether or not the idea is in line with the rules of small talk.If you don't, take a deep breath and swallow the thought and then talk about it with someone with a similar viewpoint.

Keep in mind that there are other perspectives.

It is also essential to remember that not all people are likely to hold an identical view to your own.As was previously mentioned in a previous chapter often we fall into the habit of conversing with those who share the same views that we do own.This is why whenever a situation arises in which you're conversing with people with an opinion that is different from yours It can appear to be a little obnoxious or foreign.This is a situation that shouldn't stop you from engaging with someone through small talk.Again there are people who do not have willing to follow the guidelines of small talk.Some individuals may make a point of imposing their opinions on you even if you've not asked for it. However, it doesn't mean you have to take action to back.If you're honest is the case, you should know that you'd prefer to not be a positive person to the person you are talking to who is talking to you and not portray yourself as someone who's unfriendly or rude.

Open-End Questions

If you think that the conversation is going well and you'd like to to know someone more open-ended questions are an effective strategy can be used to make the conversation less dull or mundane.Again be aware that the word "open-ended" doesn't necessarily refer to controversial or biased.These kinds of open-ended questions can be used to help you to meet the person you're talking to a little better without having to inject your opinion on the situation.Some questions to be thinking about asking are open-ended , yet light in nature. These include the following:

"Are you anticipating something this week or over the weekend?"

"Did you have anything interesting to do today?"

"What's funny thing that's occurred to you recently?"

Although these questions might seem to be a bit corny and posed when written in the form of a textbook, you are certainly able to alter these questions to your way of speaking.You don't have to consider these questions as being identical to the ice-breaker questions were asked in summer camp or in school Instead, you should take these questions naturally as you are able to.

Discover Something New

Finally, as you go along the path of building your communication skills, which include the ability to talk in small groups It could be an excellent idea to try the best you can to get some new information that you've learned from every conversation your have.You could make your endeavor as formal or casual as you'd like.For instance, if you are worried about your abilities in small-talking You can keep a notebook that documents the new skills you've acquired or an assessment you've made of yourself about how you can be better in the next conversation your have.Being open also implies accepting the idea of self-improvement.

Chapter 9: Minimal Talk For People Who Aren't

Some of the advice that I shared on how to talk small for social anxiety are applicable to those who are introverts, but it's not exactly the same. If you're an introvert, that implies that you don't have an anxiety that you're trying to conquer. This simply means that you'd rather be in your home and watching your favourite show or having a drink with your pals instead of going to an enormous party.

Do not let the reality you're introverted cause you to claim that you cannot improve at something. Imagine the most extrovert person you've ever met. Wouldn't it be great to have someone who was better at listening and retaining stories that they've previously been told? It's true!

The reason you are unable to control your Introversion is not due to anxiety

The great thing about the introverted lifestyle and not suffering from the social anxiety that comes with it is you're scared of social situations. You simply find them exhausting. Like me, when I was at University. It wasn't because I was anxious or uneasy about myself I simply wanted to be at the library, reading an article.

This is a great benefit for you since all you have to work on is the conversation skills you've been discussing, and you'll be enjoying the gathering. If you meet an intimate group of people talking about topics you enjoy and enjoy, you'll enjoy a lot.

Think about learning to talk in small groups as small obstacles that eventually bring you to something much more enjoyable. It's the same as learning how to play the guitar. It's not easy at first. the instrument and it causes pain to your fingers however once you get past that phase, you'll be able to have lots of enjoyment.

Do not put too much pressure on yourself.

There are plenty of people who are extroverts in the crowd who are sure to enjoy being the focal point of the attention. The best part is that you can watch the party at a safe distance. Marching in the direction of people who are interesting to you and immediately beginning conversations with them is not always necessary. You can stay focused on your own goals by being relaxed in all things and soon people will begin to gather towards you without having to do anything. If you're not comfortable sharing too much about yourself when you're in an interview, just do not.

Be sure to add more detail to your answers

If someone asks you how your day went and you are asked to answer, "It was good." Then, you can respond by saying, "It was good, however, I would have liked to have been home earlier after work. You know, I need to take a break. Sometimes you require that alone time, don't ya think?" That way, you can let the other person inquire further or expand on the discussion. This method helps keep the conversation from becoming unproductive and a lot of substance can be added to the conversation as it develops.

For introverts, this will be the one place where it will be more difficult for you to succeed. It's okay to speak about yourself, it's ok.Don't immediately assume that you're boring In reality, the majority of people enjoy listening to other people and hearing their tales.

Avoid pondering over blunders

I spoke about this in the previous chapter, but I I wanted to reiterate this as my struggle is with it issue a frequently and am an introvert. It's important to remember that once something is done, so there's no point in reliving the past. Make your thoughts more realistic with these questions

Do I just over-analyse the events?

Do I put too much pressure on myself?

Does this self-analysis lift my spirits or is it dragging me down?

Take a break when you feel you are analysing yourself to excessively. You'll find that the most beneficial thing of self-reflection is that it allows you to can change your own self-image, but you must ensure it that it doesn't force you alter your nature.

Make sure to take time to recover

The pressure of professional and social obligations isn't easy for introverts. Therefore, it is important to periodically take a break to recharge. The majority of introverts feel tired when they've had too many chats with too many individuals particularly if they are engaging in conversational exchanges, so it's okay to recharge for a couple of minutes by grabbing an alcoholic drink or going outside.

The most important thing I'm trying to emphasize is to not spend too much time on an interruption. If you're in a social gathering and you leave the room and you're exactly where you'd like be, alone in your mind to think. This will be comfortable and you'll be drawn to staying there. The sight of the crowd of people is likely to be a lot more intimidating and you'll wish to go home. Therefore, keep your breaks brief and set your own recharge time to be scheduled for the time you arrive home.

The difference in talking to an extrovert and. an introvert.

One thing to keep in mind is that the tone of the conversation can alter depending on whether you're an extrovert or an introvert. The pros and cons are there for each, and you may find that you prefer one over the other.

Extrovert

If you're talking to someone who is people who are extroverts, it will be much easier to engage them and inspire them to continue talking. This could relieve a lot of stress off since you only have just ask them one straightforward question, and they'll likely talk about it for a long time. They are also naturally adept at filling in the silence, so you can rest assured that they'll make up for any gaps.

This all sounds wonderful for an introvert, but the negative is that your enthusiasm levels are likely to be a lot lower than an extrovert's. That means that they will be bored quickly and decide to switch to having a conversation with a different person. The best way to stay away from this is to be aware of the primary ingredient in small talk, which is excitement. If you attempt to exaggerate your response to what they're saying you will get interest and want to keep talking.

Introvert

The best thing about speaking to an person who is an introvert, they'll know what you're saying. They're likely to not enjoy talking about themselves, so it's likely they'll want to make the conversation something more profound than an extrovert. This is a great thing for you since you'll be able to have an enjoyable and engaging conversation. Chances of making a great friend from this situation is also very significant because you are communicating on a more personal level.

The drawback of speaking to someone who is an introvert don't know is that the conversation may get stuck quickly. If you're not able to find an intimate conversation that both of you enjoy You'll be trapped in awkward small talk that doesn't move forward. Be aware of this and the topics you choose to discuss and the questions you ask will be much more effective than your body language and listening abilities. You'll have to become more comfortable speaking and filling the gaps.

Once you've got an understanding of the way the conversation might take place with both extroverts and introverts, you're aware of the strategies to put in your purse at what moment.

Think about abandoning the game

One of the most significant changes in your attitude towards small talk is to let go of your expectations for any outcome. The moment I ceased the need to fulfill all expectations to become my friends that I began making connections. It's not always going to go as you'd like. There are times when you feel like your small talk is taking you nowhere , and you begin wondering if there's a reason to speak to anyone at all. The issue isn't with the small talk, but rather your attention on the result that must be diverted to other areas. Instead of having a goal in mind, if you engage with people out of simply curiosity, you'll not only make new acquaintances but will also appreciate the experience. If you're not "outcome driven," you will end having what you desire.

Chapter 10: Tip To Achieving Success In Small Talk

How do I start a conversation?

When you initiate an exchange or conversation by speaking, you are communicating your thoughts, feelings thoughts, opinions, and ideas to a person or group of people.

The process of starting a conversation with someone could be one of the toughest aspects of communicating. It is possible that you can speak to people in a matter of minutes and conversing with others is like forcing yourself to do things you do not like. Don't fret There are a few tips that can assist you in learning how to begin a conversation with anyone. In this article I will discuss how to effectively begin and have a conversation with anyone.

Start a conversation with nearly all of them:

Let the person know that you value their conversations

It is possible to turn a stranger into a close friend in making sure he feels relaxed and showing you take interest in the things he says. Also, you show the importance of his opinion to you. If the person standing in front of your thinks you're talking only in order to listen, he'll be immediately turned off. Turn your body to look at the other person and keep eye contact, but not becoming too focused. Give the person plenty of privacy, yet show that you're attentive to the other person.

Let the person know that your thoughts are valuable. If he starts to talk about it instead of speaking about something you actually would like to discuss.

Name someone's name at least once or twice after learning it.

If someone talks first, make sure you nod your head to show you're paying attention.

You can ask questions but not to question the individual

Sometimes a conversation starts with questions, but the person with whom you're speaking to should not think that you are interrogating him as police. Be sure to not ask questions to him without offering feedback. Inquiring too much will make the person you are talking to feel uncomfortable, and he'll try to find ways to cut off the conversation.

If you notice that you've asked numerous questions try making an ode to it. Tell yourself, "Sorry... the interview has ended." and then continue talking about something else.

Find out about the person's interests or hobbies, but not about his hopes and goals.

Talk about something you enjoy. Do not ask what his thoughts are on the most recent tragedy, or inquire about his work hours. Let the person be awed by the topic of conversation and also the your conversation.

Make it amusing

Being funny doesn't mean you must perform an act of stand-up Just make a few jokes and share an interesting story to make them feel more comfortable. You'll be amazed to learn that telling jokes or stories that are funny can encourage others to share their stories. Everyone enjoys laughing and having fun makes others feel at ease. This is the most effective way to calm those who are stressed and engage them in conversation.

Make use of your cleverness to grab a people's attention. Make sure you're adept at navigating the crowd and you are comfortable with wordplay funny jokes, clever quips, and general conversation.

If you've got a truly funny story, tell it so long as it's not too brief. Do not tell a lengthy story that you've never tried before or you might be a failure.

Ask open-ended questions

What is open questions? These are ones that require more than a simple yes or no to get an answer. Questions that are open ended allow people to go into more detail and leads to a conversation or small talk between two people. These kinds of questions allow the conversation to develop and expand, in contrast to questions that have no answer.

Be sure that the question is left open enough.

It is important to recognize when a conversation isn't going according to plan. If someone is giving you a either a yes or no response to questions that demand a greater than a few seconds, it means that they isn't interested in engaging with you.

Know what to avoid doing

There are numerous ways to stop a great conversation before it's had the chance to develop. If you're trying to figure out how to start a great conversation, there are some basic tips to be aware of at the start.

Do not divulge too much of your personal details. Don't discuss your painful breakups, that weird redness on your back or even how you're starting to doubt if anyone else you know truly loves you. This is for those who really know you very well.

Don't inquire about anything that causes him to feel uncomfortable. Allow the person to talk about his loved ones and their careers or his health.

Do not waste your time discussing yourself. While joking about your self and sharing some personal details may make someone feel comfortable, however if you're talking about yourself and only about how amazing you are, they is bound to drop interest.

Be attentive- Make sure you remember the person's name and job title, or any crucial information that they reveal within five minutes. This will make them feel like you are truly interested. When someone says his name, repeat it loudly and you'll be more likely to be able to recall the name.

Begin conservation by introducing different types of people.

Engage in the conversation with someone you're interested in

If you've come across someone you like and you want to have a conversation, it is important to draw the person's attention to you, by offering the conversation to life with something fresh, funny and engaging, as well as engaging in a flirty way. If you're starting conversations with someone you enjoy how you express things is as important as the words you say. Maintain eye contact and direct your body in the direction of the person in front of you, showing the person that you're paying attention. Here are some excellent ways to begin conversations with someone you love.

If you're attending a party, discuss about the music being played. This gives you a topic to discuss, regardless of whether you like or hate the music.

If you're having a having a drink at a bar ask the bartender to recommend drinks. You may approve of the drink if you enjoy the taste. However in the event that you didn't like the drink, then you can make use of this to begin an exchange and explore different drinks.

Inform the person about their hobbies without being overly invasive Ask her what she enjoys to do to have fun during the weekend.

Don't discuss jobs. This can be a turnoff. You'll be able to go back to it later.

Engage in an exchange of ideas with a possible friend

If you happen to establish a friendship with someone you have met or you're hanging out with friends and would like to get to know your friend's person better, you must be interested in him or her, but without being overbearing. Use humor and discover more about the person.

Maintain a positive attitude: Begin with a positive statement and talk about sports (if the person is interested in sports) or a different topic you think he or she is interested in. Don't make yourself look self-deprecating, or complain immediately.

Discuss your neighborhood, because people are proud of the place they call home as well as the things they enjoy to do in the neighborhood. You can then get more personal and discuss the areas where you used to reside.

Find out what the person enjoys doing to have amusement. You might discover that you have common subjects of interest.

Do not talk about yourself too much. Make sure you're talking to each other with the same frequency.

If you have friends who are common and you have a common friend, ask them what they know about the common friend.

Engage in an informal conversation with a colleague

Engaging in a conversation with a coworker is somewhat difficult than beginning conversations with a possible acquaintance, lover or friend as there are certain boundaries which should not be crossed within the workplace. However, you can remain positive and discuss your personal life as much as you need to in order to engage in lively conversations.

Ask your colleague to talk about their family. Everyone loves to talk about their families. Therefore, it is logical to casually inquire about how their family is doing.

Discuss what you're planning to do over the weekend. If you're working with each other, you can arrange your weekend getaway or an outing to unwind and enjoy yourself.

Do not talk about work all the time If you're not in the middle of conversations with your coworker as you have work-related concerns; be open about your humanity and discuss your family, friends and other interests instead of talking about your project or your reports.

Begin to talk with an entire group of people

Conversations with a large group of people could be a little tricky. The most secure way to begin an exchange is to find an area of agreement. Although it isn't easy to ensure that everyone is comfortable and bring something towards the dialogue, make an effort to involve the most people possible by keeping it simple and easy.

Poke fun at yourself. This is a fantastic technique, especially when you're engaging in conversation with people who may know you, but do not have a great relationship with each other. Make sure that people are laughing at you or teasing them and they'll be well on the way to making a connection.

Be sure to address the whole group, not just one or two individuals. If you expressly focus your comments on one person, the others may feel excluded.

Start with a tale of the one thing you hate about yourself, and others will surely take part.

Find out what the people in the group could have in common, and make them the subject of discussion.

Always be prepared to share your thoughts

"Always always have something interesting to speak about. A person who is able to speak his mind and is not known to speak until he's had been heard." Dale Carnegie

How many of us are anxious when it's most vital? Conversation that is effective and keeps others entertained isn't simple. Conversation is among the methods of communication. We get scared when do not have words during a conversation.

At times, even when you are at a loss of words, you could want to chat for hours about something. But, having some meaningful topics to discuss could transform your life. Therefore, it's important for you to engage in meaningful conversations with others as it helps them feel more comfortable and allows them to become acquainted with you.

There are a myriad of scenarios in which two or more persons could meet for a chat such as the wedding reception, a job interview, or just hanging out in the Jacuzzi.

What are the commonalities in these scenarios? In all of these scenarios, there are people trying to speak to one another. When you are in a situation where an exchange of words can increase the value of the meeting but you are often left out because you don't have something to say.

How do you engage in how to engage in Small Talk?

There's nothing too small in Small Talk. While you might think the purpose of small talk is an excuse to have fun or avoid awkwardness, think twice. Many of the best friendships and relationships began with a brief chat regarding the weather. Small talk can not only aid in building an emotional relationship with someone else however, it is also an essential skill that will help you in your professional world. I've already mentioned these as stories and an actual incident in the earlier chapter.

Small Talk Small Talk: the "Who, What, Where What, When, and Why?"

Who creates Small Talk?

Like me, you and those with numerous relationships participate on Small Talk. People of all ages take part within Small Talk especially when they don't know one another. While we teach our children to not talk with strangers, grown-ups are required to at least say one or two words when they are in certain situations. Friends of friends Office employees who may not be great friends, but who work within the same department are the ones who you can talk to on Small Talk.

Customer service representatives such as waitresses and waitresses, as well as hairdressers and receptionists frequently engage in Small Talk with customers.

What can people talk about while in Small Talk?

There are some "safe" subjects that people typically create Small Talk about. Most people discuss weather, current events news, sports. If you have something in the same both of you you may discuss it as well. For instance, if the bus is full and there aren't any seating is available do you be able to discuss reasons for this?

Negative remarks are not allowed when it comes to Small Talk. Do not discuss personal issues or personal issues of other people. It's not a good idea to discuss topics that other people aren't at ease with or even at all.

Where can people have fun engaging in Small Talk?

People can engage in Small Talk anywhere but there are specific areas where it is popular to talk. The majority of the time, Small Talk occurs in places in which people are waiting for something. For instance, you could converse with someone who is sitting beside you, waiting for the bus to arrive , or with those waiting to catch a train in an area that is waiting for trains at a station.

Also, people engage in Small Talk with other passengers when traveling long distances. At a doctor's appointment, in which patients wait for their turn to see the doctor and are engaged on Small Talk with other people. At social gatherings like weddings, parties or gatherings participants take part with Small Talk with the hosts and guests.

When should people be engaging with each other in Small Talk?

The most popular moment when it is most common for Small Talk to occur is the first time you meet people on a certain day. For instance, if you meet your colleague in the office lounge , you may greet them and talk about the sport or the weather. However, if you see him again this same date, you could simply smile or be silent.

Another great time to engage in Small Talk is during a break during a presentation or meeting or presentation, when there's nothing significant happening. It is also important to be aware of the signal that the other person is asking for the conversation to cease.

What is the reason people are involved in small talk?

There are many reasons people participate with Small Talk. One of the primary, and most evident reason one is breaking the Ice. Another reason is to have fun or to know someone better. This is the reason it's popular engaging with Small Talk when you are waiting for something or someone. Many people use small talk to show respect. It's possible that you don't feel like talking to anyone at a social gathering however it appears odd to sit in a quiet corner and don't interact with other people.

If someone introduces you someone else, you may not know much about the person, so to be courteous you display the desire to get to know the other person better and take part into Small Talk with others.

Do's and Don'ts for engaging in Small Talk

Do's:

It is important to ensure that there is a genuine interest in a subject before you begin talking about it.

Make sure to stick with topics that are upbeat.

Make sure you balance the amount of speaking and listening.

Find out what others are discussing.

You should be prepared to discuss things you have no idea about.

Bring back a former acquaintance.

Don'ts:

Engage in endless talk about shops or gossip from the industry when other people are in the room.

Talk about other guests.

Keep to one place or talk to only one person.

Take a look over the shoulder of someone while you speak to them.

Make snap judgements that are negative regarding individuals you encounter.

You can count on other people to carry the discussion.

How can I restart the conversation?

There are occasions where you'll realize that your conversation is at an end. This is the situation where, during the course of a discussion in a group everyone ends up having a discussion and arguing with the other instead of to the group. This scenario is also referred to by the name of "fish market" since you don't know what's happening as everyone is trying to articulate their perspective.

The difference is that in Small Talk, you come to a point at which you don't have anything to discuss and find yourself with an unfocused expression on your face. In discussions in groups, the things can go off the rails.

In any case it is essential to offer your Small Talk a small boost. Also the conversation must be restarted so you can carry on talking.

Take a look at the first example I mentioned at the beginning in the novel. Steve has been waiting on an announcement regarding delay in the departure time of his flight and then he engages in Small Talk with his family. Instead of the announcement about departure, if an announcement of a delay for the next flight is made, what should Steve do? Should he keep the conversation with his family? What happens if he leaves the family members and went to the gate for boarding for the flight and then an decision was made?

It is possible to think of many scenarios that could take place at the airport.

At present take into consideration it was just before Steve said goodbye to his family. He was then required to be able to speak about. He could not afford to stay in the dark and make fun of the whole situation.

If you were at Steve's home how would you do in this scenario ? announcement that the plane will be leaving after a half-hour while the plane is cleaned to be ready for departure.

How can you revive your conversation with your family?

Here are some possible options I have in mind.

Steve is likely to make an argument that the airline officials wanted him not to fly out and have given him time with his family. He could also have a little fun in with Jen and play Adrian for a bit more.

Steve is also able the gift of an chocolate bar for Adrian or even by the family for with a coffee.

These are just a few ways you can restart the conversation with these people.

Chapter 11: Talk The Talk

The act of speaking is among the primary ways humans, as individuals communicate with the people we come across in our daily lives. By using words, we are able to describe our experiences, express emotions, or even discuss subjects that interest us or are concerning. Communication is a vital ability that everyone should acquire in order to succeed socially today in our society.

While there are many different methods of communication talking and using words is the most simple and understandable method of letting others know what's going on. It doesn't matter if it's with your family member, acquaintance, friend or a stranger, to talk with them the conversation will almost certainly be held. It may range from banter that is meaningless to heated debate. Depending on the person the conversation is taking place with will influence the way we interact with that person. For most of us, it's more comfortable to engage in an exchange with someone who is familiar or someone we've met previously, than someone who is completely new to us. The thought of speaking loudly to anyone, much less to someone you have never met, can be unnerving, stressful or create anxiety for certain people.

It's not the scenario for all. I, for instance, enjoy the chance to talk to the person waiting in line behind me at the supermarket or even on the lift at work. I've always believed that I could gain something new from each of the people I meet, as long as I am willing to.

My husband however will not just avoid talking to strangers unless absolutely necessary and also look at me as if I'm an insane person whenever I do it myself while out with him. He isn't sure about this at all and that's fine. As I discussed the reasons why he is so averse to him and he told me that he feels anxious and unsure because he doesn't know what to discuss with someone he's never seen before. It's much more comfortable and easier for him to remain his own thoughts to his personal space.

Communication through conversations plays an essential function in our daily lives and there's no need it should be thought to be difficult or trigger any type of anxiety-driven emotions. In the college setting, one of the compulsory classes that is usually part of the standard academic requirement are Speech also known as Public Speaking. The classes typically concentrate on speaking to large groups of people or delivering a speech but there's some merit about being able to communicate publicly in general. It is essential to teach a class in how to have an engaging conversation with any person.

To make it clear for those who aren't familiar with about small talk, which is what we'll discuss in this book can be described as the act of engaging in conversations when nothing of significance is being discussed. It could happen while taking the train back home after work at the end in the workday, or waiting around at the table waiting to have the food ready, or waiting on the line to go to the banking.

There are many ways to follow to have an effortless and fluid conversation with any person you encounter. It could be someone you've talked to hundreds of times previously, or it could it be your first experience you've talked to you, yet the result is the same: a successful conversation. These guidelines include following fundamental rules of conversation and treating people like you've known them for years, paying attention and interpreting the words of the person you are telling them, and then following up on what you've stated you'd do. A pleasant experience in which everyone leaves feeling more informed after having learned something, and comprehending what they've received is the ultimate goal of any communication that is successful. It's ok

Conversation can mean more than the exchange of information between individuals who interact with each other. Since small talk plays an important role in our daily lives, if we adhere to the basic rules of conversation and guidelines, we can ensure that both ourselves as well as the person we are communicating with are making the most of the conversation and the experience.

Conversations and discussions, when conducted with an open-minded mind, provide us with the chance to discover something new that we've not heard of or considered before, particularly when we interact with strangers. Listening is essential to help turn a simple conversations into lengthy discussions and the start of a new friendships, or even a new business relationship. If you take the time to listen to what your counterpart is saying and listen, you give them to expand discussions in other areas as they chat.

What I'm going claim isn't something you learned in school, let me be the first person to tell you that actions speak more than words. I'm not certain who originally believed this however they were definitely right. There is no way for anyone to be convinced the fact that you're a trustworthy person until you perform the things you say you will do. It is crucial that your actions match your words when talking about small things if it will be more than it being a conversation. Conversations with friends can result in huge things, such as new friendships or business concepts and mergers, or just personal experiences to educate us or that million-dollar idea that's been floating around in the haze.

With a few simple guidelines and some helpful tips small talk can be transformed into something productive no matter who you're having it with. After having read this book, you should feel more confident and confident in beginning talking to strangers, friends or relative, and everything in between, as if they were one and same. Conversations with strangers can be a bit intimidating regardless of whether you are speaking to the group or with one person, particularly in the event that you do not have a lot of experience socially. Making small talks is a skill that can be taught, and turning your little talk to something that is more profitable is a skill which can be developed.

Conversational Commandments

Certain fundamentals must be followed to transform a conversational nonsense into a positive conversation for all parties that is. It doesn't matter whether you're talking with an acquaintance or a stranger This makes these suggestions more straightforward to follow since they're universal. In this guide, we'll use these tips as conversational rules. The first thing we'll discuss is the most important thing to know for having a successful conversation regardless of the person you are interacting by Listening.

Listening is the most important aspect of communication because it ensures that all participants are talking with each other, rather than at one another. This also means that the participants attain an knowledge about one another as well as the subject which is being discussed. If the most difficult thing to deal with when talking has to do with not being able to decide what topic to discuss, then listening to what your partner is telling you is a great place to begin. It doesn't matter if you're talking about the subject of their choice or providing suggestions on a issue they're facing the only way you'll be able to be of assistance is to simply listen first.

Two other suggestions that are closely linked to the listening component of conversations. They are paying attention to details while waiting for other person to end before they speak. These two tips are crucial in communicating with the person you're talking to know that you have actually listened and understood the topic they're discussing. This doesn't mean that you thought the subject was going to be fascinating It just means that you paid attention.

Being genuine is important since it lets someone feel that you are genuinely interested. Being attentive allows you to focus on the particulars of the words spoken by the speaker. The information can be used to keep the conversation going. It doesn't matter if have a conversation with your mother or a lady who is standing in front of in the line at the banks. If you use their words to trigger the words you use and the conversation will be bound to keep going. Everyone is interested in what they say in their personal words.

Another great tip to pay attention to the minute details is remembering what the name of the other person is, and using it in the conversation. There's nothing more likely to make someone feel more at ease with you more than using their name when talking to them. There is a certain level of familiarity that is associated with it. Consider your personal experiences when someone calls you with a name.

It's the little things that play the biggest impact in turning conversations from a casual conversation or something else. If you allow your partner to complete what they want to say before adding in the discussion, you not just show that you're a gentleman as well as make them more likely to think about and appreciate your words because they think that you actually been listening to them. The extent to which you've listened is another matter, however, by giving the other person an impression of listening already turned your conversation to something important to them. If you've done this honestly, then perhaps it's for you as well.

Another reason to let them finish talking is you don't end any possible topics of conversation that they were going to bring up prior to when you reacted with your opinion. In order to simplify things simply allow them to talk before you speak. How do you expect to decide what to say when you begin talking before they've completed speaking? It's not that easy be able to, and the conversation will be over soon after interruption.

It might sound simple, but it's crucial enough to bring up. Be sure to be understood when you're talking. Every aspect that you say, from your tone to speed, or volume could be the defining element of conversation, so ensure that your audience is able to comprehend and hear what you're saying to them. It's not worth talking, whether it's casual conversation or an important discussion, if one of the participants does not comprehend the topic being discussed. If you're speaking too fast, you should slow down. If you're talking in a quiet manner, say something! Be sure to pronounce your thoughts and explain to the person you're speaking to, if they appear in a state of confusion or are willing to ask what you're talking about.

A second, and obvious, method is to maintain eye contact when you are in any kind of conversation, whether it's small or big. There's nothing that can cause you to appear more uninterested in what someone else is saying than when you're gazing everywhere or not paying attention to anything in addition to the words they are saying. It doesn't matter if they're speaking to you or talking to them. Be sure to look them directly in the eyes while the conversation is going on.

As there are ways to make sure that a conversation is successful, there are some things you should avoid when doing this. One of them is to ensure that everyone is on the same page. This can be achieved by a variety of ways if you are looking to transform a conversation into something more substantial. First, you must ensure that the subject is relevant to both people. If the person you are talking to is an unknown person or one whom you don't know well, the best option is to discuss them. Once you've completed your research by listening to the person's conversation and paying close attention to the important particulars (including your name) You should at a minimum have a couple of thoughts of whether you should ask the person about themselves or about topics that they might be interested in. When you let them speak for a few minutes and listen to them, you will discover something you can and discuss with at most an interest level that is moderate.

Another method to keep the conversation going is to make sure you don't rebut what you hear from the other party. This means that you let them finish what they want to say without trying to outdo them each time, or so it seems. Be respectful to them, especially in the case of a stranger. If it's someone you've just met or are becoming acquainted with and get to know, allowing them an opportunity to show off their talents (even even if it's just during a conversation) could make a difference. The conversation shouldn't feel like a game to anyone involved. It should be a mutual participation from everyone involved and be enjoyable for all and for everyone.

Nobody would like a conversation that is one-sided therefore, do not allow it to turn into only one. If you notice that the person you're speaking with has stopped engaging within the dialogue, you can ask them a question that will engage them again or shift the topic to one they may be more inclined to talk about. If you don't allow yourself to continue on for too long and putting in the effort in order to create a conversation that is exciting or pleasant for the other person you've accomplished your job of showing that you are genuinely interested.

Chapter 12: Learn To End Any Conversation The Power Of No

Your energy and time are the most valuable and precious resources, so treat them accordingly.

You need to learn how to tell"no..

Have you ever found yourself in an environment that you are forced to keep a conversation going even though you sincerely would like it to be over?

It is important to note that you're able to quickly leave any conversation, while others think you're listening intently.

I've done it. Many times. In addition, I've chosen to listen to these conversations since I had been taught how to be courteous and kind to anyone. In further detail when I was a kid I received that the Golden Rule of Morality - "Treat people in the manner you would want to be treated".

Unfortunately, I wasn't instructed that the rule can be applied in various contexts.

Imagine a situation where I was talking with an individual who's company I don't find enjoyable, is it fair for me to continue the conversation? Do I have the right to confine them to me, my boring self, thus preventing them from interacting with other individuals whose company they could prefer? It's not fair.

The fact is that I personally wouldn't wish for people to continue to talk with me simply because they are feeling they are sorry for me. What I would like to see in this scenario is for them to make the effort to politely leave the conversation. This shows that they are aware of both their time as well as my time.

As a result of the realization that I had, I began studying how to be an improved and more sensitive person when I speak to others, which will help not only my friends but as well myself.

We are introverts and find socializing extremely energetic and since every energy joule counts and is important, it is suggested that you make wise use of them. If you do not, you'll end up exhausted and battered by social interactions.

Let's suppose that you're in a discussion where you have asked the right questions, but the other person is giving you a few superficial responses. If you notice the apprehension of answers that, although you know the meaning of, you don't feel any need for. It becomes clear that the person you're talking to isn't the kind of person you'd want to engage in conversations with.

In simple terms, to reduce your energy consumption divide your conversations into two sections that are: BEFORE you can tell whether you are a fan of a particular person and AFTER you've got enough details.

Before you do that, you're giving this person the chance to shine to ask the appropriate open-ended questions. You are also paying attention and trying to understand the reason behind the person's remarks or responses.

After: What's your exit plan for this discussion. What should you do if you've made the decision to leave?

Conversations revolve around the mindsets and viewpoints. Bestir yourself positively. Do not feel guilty about ending the conversation because it isn't going anywhere. While all conversations should end at some point, you must ensure that the conversation has a purpose. It doesn't matter if it's for enjoyment or enjoyment or networking, it should be a learning experience. If you find the conversation to be unfocused, meaningless or you're tired or bored, never forget that you're free to quit. Nobody is obligated to stay there. The decision to remain there will not benefit you nor anyone else. person(s).

A common-sense rule of thumb It is not sensible nor wise to be blunt and honest in the exit. It is important to always remain polite. Your words must be clear however your actions must be considerate.

Chapter 13: Reassurances To Self-Confidence And Confidence

It is crucial to know about the power of affirmations and how beneficial they can be for your life. These are short but profound statements that typically create similar images in a person's mind, which are motivating invigorating, stimulating and inspiring. This particular part focuses on the ability of you to increase your self-confidence and self-esteem. affirmations can be an essential tool. It is true that whatever causes you to feel down in your self-esteem or makes you feel like you don't value your self-worth mostly comes in your thinking. Here are some excellent affirmations that alter your thoughts in a manner that makes you feel more confident. It is important to make a list of specific affirmations that , if used often will not only enhance confidence in yourself, but also allow you to develop personally.

I am loved and respected.

I am a person who has the potential to make great strides in my life

I am an exceptional and talented person

I am making progress on improving my self-confidence and confidence.

The great aspect to me is I'm always solution and logical.

I've never felt the need to ask approval from others.

I appreciate and value all aspects of my life.

I am able to fill my mind filled with positive, healthy and loving thoughts .

I've decided to be in the moment.

I am sorry for me and other people for the past regrets and hurts.

I am making tremendous progress in my professional career.

My family and friends are my best friends. me to death.

I let go of any negative thoughts or emotions.

I find the best in myself as well as in others.

I am on my way to progress and growth.

I enjoy talking to people, as they inspire me to be the best version of me.

I always exercise self-love

Through change allows me to improve and accomplish more in my life.

My life is shifting as I had expected.

I will never let anything cause me to lose my joy.

My passion for people as well as for me has allowed me to truly improve and to move past my failures and pain.

I have the qualities to be successful.

I'm very intelligent both on the inside and the outside.

Chapter 14: Have Fun, People Love Jokes However, Don't Overdo It.

The act of making jokes makes chats with strangers much more fun. It also increases the length of conversation. People who are funny can have their way with others. A lot of them will listen to them even if the topics they are discussing are not very serious.

It is possible that you are not an original joker, however you can improve your skills. It can be a benefit when starting conversations with strangers. Have fun with the topics that you're talking about. Humor is an excellent way to break up the monotony of your conversation.

Small talk isn't something people like, however the ability to make it enjoyable by making a few jokes. It's difficult for anyone not to enjoy a good joke. This is a method that keeps the conversation moving. Conversations with friends often lead to unexpected outcomes that we don't expect.

It could lead to an employment opportunity, a spouse or even a great business deal. It's only going to be the case if the conversation is able to last a bit longer. Jokes are an excellent way to keep the other person entertained.

But, being too funny can make the other person believe you're not serious. The primary purpose behind comedy is to have fun in the mood. But, this shouldn't be the main focus of the whole conversation.

Veer away from personal jokes. For example, making jokes about the physical attributes of the person you are talking to could deter them from paying attention. It is important keeping the discussion flowing without disturbing the other person.

If your entire conversation revolves around jokes, the listener might feel that they are being sucked into a whimper. To be successful in a small talk, have an intelligent conversation, and then make it interesting by adding some funny stories. There is no way to get it wrong.

Chapter 15: Small Talk Society

After we have examined the different precautions you should be aware of in order to have a safe and intimate conversations, let's take a consider the ways you can inspire others to do the same.

We will look at the different ways you can begin doing immediately to start your small-talk agenda.

Advertisements can be posted

You can post advertisements in your online social network profiles and invite friends to a one-on-one conversations. While your friends will be accepted, you must convince them to join your acquaintances, who are not familiar to you. They'll increase the number of friends you have. It is also possible to invite your friends and neighbors to join as members. Together, you'll gather a large number of people who interact and will help you increase your circle of friends.

Form a group

After you've had a conversation with everyone, distribute forms and inquire if any of them would like to join an informal group. A small-talk group can be made up of people who would like to chat with strangers, and grow their circle of friends. When you have the right number of names may create a group and hold regular gatherings. It is possible to assign a role to each person and designate a specific space such as a cafe or mall where they can engage in conversation. The group could also be involved in encouraging new members to join your group, which will build a large small-talking base.

Do it with others

The group could work together and devise efficient ways to talk about small things. They will be able to come up with numerous ways they can enhance themselves as well as improve their communication and social abilities. The group is especially beneficial for introverts since it can encourage them to open up and participate in small-talk activities. It is also a good idea to encourage children to take part and help them develop solid communication and language abilities. This can help them make more new friends, and will help them appreciate that it's important to maintain a huge number of friends.

Expand

When you've got enough people in your group you can grow the group and then start to spread the word to relatives or friends living elsewhere. It is possible to ask them to establish their own discussion groups, and one day you'll be able to establish the same kind of group all across the country.

Travel

It is also possible to organize excursions for your group. You can enjoy local trips or if have a policy for payment members and you want to provide them with international travel. Traveling with your group, you'll get the opportunity to meet different people from around the globe. You'll be able to build a strong friendship base that includes individuals from all walks of life, faith and age group, as well as sexual orientation, etc.

Chapter 16: What You Can Do To Enhance Your Charisma

can distinguish leaders and executives, as well as divine beings.

In the past, supernatural aspects were believed to be associated with charisma. It was believed to be an act of the divine being who lives in heaven, providing people with the ability and power to guide others. The definition that we use today of charisma includes magnetic, charisma, confidence as well as personal capability, and the ability to draw others around a goal or vision. People are considered charismatic when they can convince others especially when an overall vision is being propagated. Leaders tend to act by engaging in a manner that draws the attention of their followers. A very effective techniques to recognize how charismatic leaders are is the ability to grace. Grace is a strategy which plays an important role in changing the way that charisma is a key factor in leadership.

The term "charm" is extensively utilized in the social sciences and religions, and is defined and used in different ways. Charisma is, however, a rare trait that is found in a small number of people who have the ability to easily influence other people. The charismatic display the rare qualities of assertiveness, calmness authority as well as authenticity and peace. They also have amazing abilities in communicating.

Characteristics of Charisma

In many instances you will meet charismatic individuals, however, you will not know their personality. People who are great communicators will always get your attention and the respect of an audiences even when the situation is not ideal. They are usually characterized by a personality that are confident, optimistic and understanding, as well as respectful and genuine. They are able, competent and powerful (C.O.U.R.A.G.E). There are some people born with charismatic traits, but others develop it in their teen years. Here are a few traits of charisma.

The charisma and confidence are two of the most important characteristics. Confident people have a huge confidence in themselves, which can make other people trust them. People who are confident have a special faith in their physical and mental capability, which makes other people feel confident. They know the message they wish to convey to the crowd and typically identify themselves with people with a solid network of backing and those who trust in their abilities.

They are optimistic and aid others in seeing opportunities as an essential trait as a leader. They strive to inspire people to believe in their capabilities and perceive what they provide as being beneficial to all. The goals set by charismatic individuals are achievable and are designed to help everyone.

People who are charismatic have a way of being more attentive than they talk. Listening and understanding others is a characteristic that they place a high value on. They are comfortable in helping people feel valued and important. They speak only when necessary and spend the majority of their time listening to others.

People who are charismatic have a good understanding of their environment and viewers. They do to not offend others' opinions. They look at their surroundings and adjust their behaviour and boundaries in a way that is appropriate.

The charismatic know their own abilities and the capabilities of their peers. With this knowledge they can create realistic goals that can be achieved by all members of the group. They know what they are able to deliver and stay clear of situations that could result in the loss of other members.

Body speech that is in line with the words they speak is another feature of charismatic individuals. They are able to convince people to trust them. The movements of their bodies are displayed natural as they speak which makes them appear honest and genuine.

The charismatic are also efficient. They are focused on the credibility of the outcome they deliver. They strive to help others succeed by ensuring that they are able to deliver the message they promise. They will always strive to build an excellent reputation.

Measuring Charisma

According to research by scientists it is possible to gauge charisma by answering six questions commonly asked. It is through these questions that you determine your scores on the level of charisma you possess. These are questions like: I am someone with the charisma to speak in an environment and is able to influence others and is able to guide an entire group, makes others feel at ease, makes smiles out of people frequently, and can be a good friend to anyone. The score you receive is divided by six and the average determines your charisma level. If the average score is greater than 3.7 You are thought as more charming than the average person.

Enhancing Your Charisma

Charisma isn't necessarily an inheritance, but rather something that you can acquire and keep as time passes. Some people automatically make you feel valued and some bring a bit of charisma to the space by just walking in. Certain people are naturally charming. They have the capacity of establishing and maintaining healthy relationships . They are also able to influence others to feel good about themselves. Everyone would like to surround themselves with these people and hopes to become like them.

Being charismatic doesn't depend on your success or how well you portray yourself, what image you portray, or the way you dress. This implies that everybody is able to be charismatic. Charisma completely depends on what you do. What you do is the impression that you show to other people around you. In order to become more charismatic, be mindful of following a set of rules which will assist you achieve your desired goals. These are just a few ways to improve your charisma.

1. Always listen more than you Talk

The only thing you need to let someone know you are important is to ask questions, keeping eye contact and smiling, frowning, acknowledging, and responding in a non-verbal manner. If you are attentive to another person and they are able to tell that you are genuinely interested in them. Be sure to speak only when requested to give suggestions. A lot of talking in the hopes of giving tips makes the conversation more about you, it's not about the individual. Be sure to only speak when you have an important item to discuss and which are related to the words of the other person. This makes them aware the importance of what they're saying. is important.

2. Do not practice selective hearing.

Be open to what you hear someone trying to tell you, no matter the person they are or the degree they're at. Make sure that everyone regardless of their social standing or status feel that you have something in common. Don't pick who to listen to or whom you won't listen to.

3. Put Your Stuff Away Always

When you're talking to someone else, make sure that your attention is focused on the person you are talking to. Be sure to avoid constantly checking your phone or looking at your monitor on your computer. Refraining from distractions caused by other activities allows you to be in touch with others more easily. Being attentive can make other people feel loved and they'll always desire to be with you. People will look up to you to be a model for others.

4. Always Give Prior to Receiving - Believing you may never receive

Never think of the ways that you can benefit the other person. The focus should always be on what you're capable of offering to someone else and how useful you could be. Giving without expecting to receive anything as a reward is one of the most effective strategies to use when developing strong relationships with others. By focusing on what another person could give you will make it appear like the relationship is about you and not about the other person. So, in order to build your charm, never worry about whether you'll receive it later on.

5. Do not act self-importantly

People who are snobby and self-important are the only people that can benefit from your self-important appearance. When you are like that, people will be put off and uncomfortable when you're with them. People won't be at all when you walk into the room, but they'll be irritated and frown. It is crucial to be humble and treat all others as equals. The way to develop charisma is to be yourself and not being a fake.

6. You should be aware that other People are More Important

You are aware of your own opinions, beliefs about your points of view and views. There is nothing else you can learn from yourself, since you already know what you know and this is not as significant. You do not know the opinions of those are saying about you, or their thoughts, opinions or points of view and viewpoints are. In general, not knowing anything about people around you is more significant to you. They are important because they are numerous aspects you could learn from. Connecting and connecting with them will allow you to learn about different aspects of life and the factors that motivates them to behave in that way. In order to build a charismatic personality be sure to view others to be more valuable than you are.

7. Try to shine the spotlight on others

Always inform people about how well you did something, by giving them praise. It is important to discover what others performed and what they accomplished. To develop charisma, you must be awed by others every moment they win. This is done and make them feel that you care and are paying close attention to their accomplishments. The appreciation of other people's work makes them feel like they've accomplished something, and feel significant.

8. Be aware of Your Attitude and your Words

The words that people use when communication have an effect on the way they think and the attitude of those around them. To be more attractive, do to make yourself feel happy, excited and content. Always think about taking an optimistic attitude and employ positive words when speaking to others. It creates a sense of pride for oneself. It also helps you feel better. Make sure that your behavior does not turn others off, but instead uplifting your mood.

9. Do not discuss the shortcomings of other People

Everyone enjoys listening to the latest gossip or a bit of dirt. The issue arises when people begin to dislike the person telling the truth or sharing gossip. Always be mindful of the feelings of others. If someone informs you about something that you did to someone else, do not laugh since they could be thinking about whether you'd are doing the same thing in the absence of them. Be sure to discuss the factors that led them to behave in a particular manner and ways to stay clear of such behavior. This will portray your character as a person who values the views of others.

10. Be Prepared to Acknowledge Your Personal Defects

There is no way to be flawless, and all of us make mistakes in certain situations. To build your personality does not mean you need to be success in all things. Make sure to admit your mistakes make and take them as lessons you've learned. When you laugh about your mistakes, the people won't laugh at you, but they will be with them. People will always prefer to hang out with you since they'll always be drawn to you more.

Conversational Charisma

Every once during a conversation, you might notice that someone else does not pay the attention of you. This can be, naturally frustrating and can turn you off. Being charismatic in conversation is essential since it makes others feel that you're interested in what they communicate. Engaging fully in a conversation could be difficult however, it is crucial to be aware of how you can improve your persona. By practicing these tips, you can improve your conversational skills.

Be present in the here and present. Being present during a conversation starts with the mind. You might feel your mind isn't settled and ready to begin conversations in certain situations. If you're a person who is charismatic do your best to concentrate on the person's feelings, for example, breathing or the way they feel on their feet when on floor. Try this for just a few seconds and you'll be able to bring your attention back to the moment you connected with them.

Always ensure that you are physically fit before engaging in conversations. It is impossible to be a charming person if you think about how tight or loose the pants you're wearing are. Make sure you're extremely comfortable and are wear clothes that fit youand are stylish and flattering. Also, getting enough rest and drinking lesser or no caffeine will assist in increasing your physical well-being.

Think about setting your devices on quiet mode, or completely off to make sure they are away from your. It is possible that as you have your phone in your hand and you're constantly looking at it or check to check for updates from social media or for updates on your phone, which can make people around you feel that your attention is diverted. Disconnecting your phone aids in preventing unnecessary interruptions and lets you participate in the conversation completely.

Be careful not to fidget. This signal is thought to indicate that you're not at ease and that you feel you're in a wrong spot. Avoid checking your surroundings while the person speaking speaks. Moving around makes the other person feel your current situation in isn't ideal, and you're seeking the best one. Your attention should be focused on the present position you're in, and make sure you are paying attention to your partner.

You should not be thinking about the answer you're going to make in the event that the other person is still talking. Most people have a tendency to get involved and talk when the opportunity presents itself. The thought of what you planning to say as a response indicates that you're not paying attention to what the other person is talking about. However, it is crucial to listen carefully to the person you are talking to and think twice before making a decision. You don't have to be constantly you have to make every silence a full-on rant, but instead, take advantage of any pause that occurs. It is essential to wait several minutes before giving your response. This will show the person that you're attentive to their needs and that you're taking your time before you decide on your answer.

The advantages of charismatic leadership

A charismatic leader has numerous advantages at work. His personality is what makes employees appreciate working with a person who has excellent listening and communication abilities. Leaders who are charismatic will always provide the encouragement they need to their employees even when they face difficulties.

Employee Support - Leaders who are charismatic can provide inspiration and motivational messages to employees. They have a captivating personality that makes them feel effectively with their employees. Employees are always free to share their views and ideas because they know they will be taken in the spotlight.

Enjoyable and a more pleasant working environment If you are under the guidance of a charismatic leader employees will always be happy coming to work. The reason is that the leader can make a difficult work environment appear more appealing. Leaders who are charismatic are always convinced of the capabilities that their staff members have, thereby making them strive to be the highest level of performance they are able to. This helps to create an environment favorable to work in, thus improving the efficiency of employees.

The example of leadership to other employees The charismatic leaders are usually thought of as excellent role models for their employees. They will strive to imitate the enthusiasm, professionalism and enthusiasm of their supervisors. They eventually become potential leaders of their own. The character they build increases their chance for being promoted.

Maximum Production - When guided by a charismatic and charismatic leader employees will be focused on doing their best they can. Absenteeism or poor attitude, as well as poor work quality will be very low. Employees believe they have a leader they can trust and someone who values their well-being. Employee turnover are not a problem since they are loyal to their employer, even in a difficult circumstance they trust their boss in helping them get through the circumstances.

The charismatic leader has a preference for a continual learning process. A charismatic leader realizes that there is no such thing as completely perfect. They don't seek perfection in any activity their subordinates participate in. These leaders always provide their employees the chance to learn from failures they have made. They also learn learnings from mistakes they make. They see every mistake as an the chance to make better decisions and avoid making the same mistakes in the future.

Leadership that is charismatic gives people the opportunity to consider a different perspective on different questions. Leaders who are charismatic always seek to share their ideas and vision with others. In this way, people have the chance to think of diverse ideas on a certain topic. The people who are guided by charismatic leaders have the courage to make risks, because they are always able to give their followers a powerful message. Engaging with the thoughts and ideas of the leader creates an identity which makes them feel valued. Leaders who are charismatic believe in the value of others' thoughts and ideas, not just their own knowledge. They can influence people's lives and those of their students positively.

Being charismatic is an attribute that we must all think about studying and practicing every day. This is because it can help people build positive relationships with others as well as create an appreciation for people. The charismatic people can also help in bringing about change within society. It is because we serve as role models for other people who are around us. They are made to feel they must be considerate of others by putting everything aside and giving them our full attention. Be sure to follow the following guidelines to make you an improved person.

Chapter 17: Dealing With A Different Type Of Character From Friendly To Badass

Step-by-step instructions to learn about people's personality traits

Being aware that a portion of us are held various levels throughout the day - at home, at work, and play is a particular thing. Knowing how to use this information is a different. It is nevertheless important. Being able to differentiate characters can help us in applying our influence to improve communication, convey greater effectiveness and progress any area of play regardless of the task, whether it's getting children to play with their toys or getting a business group to reach a new target.

Scientist and creator from Los Angeles Dario Nardi Ph.D. is a researcher into the brain and maps out strategies to determine what is important to us. The findings he came across were deemed to be his neuro-scientific examinations and began the process of preparing for business began to grow.

"I'm not particularly adept at anything that requires administrative skills," Nardi says. "I am a self-observer and will do whatever it is I want to do. It is important to recognize that there are a variety of kinds of people out there and to not bind all of them to the same beliefs that I do is a huge step forward. Being able to tune in to them, acquiring the phrases they use to effectively communicate with them is a fundamental. It's all about incorporating the things I believe that a handful of people just come to regularly, but many people need to be able to adjust."

Another expert within the discipline, John D. Mayer, Ph.D., creator and professor of research on the brain within the University of New Hampshire, is an early pioneer in character and knowledge exploration brain research.

"Does it matter knowing other people's personalities?" He asks. "I believe it's important because due to the fact that each person has a zones of comfort and a zone of strength where we can be locked-in. Knowing our own areas of comfort and our personal areas of difficulty--what we're able but not prepared to do -- we can guide ourselves. If we are aware of that in the people around us, then we also can to manage ourselves within the context of them."

Nardi who has been leading the neuroscience field since 2006. He has clarified that the brain of an individual, which is the cooperative power of psyche and cerebrum--is an accumulation of forces which shape each other and form the compass we use to determine our direction.

"Individuals of various character kinds do not rely solely on different areas of their minds," Nardi says. "They are able to think and in general terms in different ways. Cerebrum as well as mindset and culture all affect one another and form a co-creative. The horse shapes the rider's choices, and the rider determines the horse's choices."

For example, Nardi observes how his subjects' cerebrums glisten when they participate in the course of their assignments. When he records his electroencephalogram, also known as an EEG is recorded, the screen changes to into a stunning, intense blue. the guinea-pig is experiencing an creative stream, achieving something that the individual is skilled of. Nardi explores ways to achieve these pinnacle moments and then continue to support these moments.

"We are in a state by one of two methods," he composes. "Regularly talent comes from the preparation. A skilled performer is into the zone when playing his music. When we're extremely skilled in our playing, closing our eyes and picturing the motion is enough to get us in the zone. At different times, top-performing minutes are linked to the character of the person that range from focusing over the past, paying total focus, observing situations, or imagining the future. In any event being constantly in the zone provides us with a rumbling slide of a flawless inventive yield."

The Journey to This Point

Therapists have investigated the hypothesis of character type since Swiss specialist/psychotherapist Carl G. Jung presented the idea during the 1910s. Jung identified four fundamental abilities which included sensing (S) and sensing (N) and thinking (T) while being able to work (F) within the outside (extroverting) or inner (introverting) environment. He employed eight psychological techniques, which he that he used as capital letters for the procedure (S N, F or F) and the lowercase letter "e" (extroverted) as well as "I" (introverting) in order to indicate the direction. Thus "Se" signifies an outgoing person that detects, and detecting is associated as a person who is committed to the outside world.

In the 1940s American writer Isabel Briggs Myers and her mother, Katharine Cook Briggs, developed The Myers-Briggs Typ Indicator (MBTI) an assessment test that was designed to make Jung's theories "justifiable and beneficial" for people's lives. The test is constantly evolving by providing users with refreshed and updated information on the mental type and its use.

"If individuals are able to contrast effectively in the things they see and how they reach resolutions, then it's just natural for them to alter their behavior to maximize their advantages and abilities, reactions or abilities." as outlined by The Myers-Briggs Foundation.

Nardi warns that preparation and ability are needed to judge and react to the character of those who are challenging. He coaches corporate coaches to are looking for confirmation in MBTI tests. "Affirmation is definitely the first step towards understanding," he says. "However regardless knowing about the different characters, even if one isn't a great fan is a good way to turn on specific lighting."

People can go online for the content according to him "and it's an actual help to individuals, no matter if you're in a workplace setting or managing a difficult teenager in high school. It offers them an extra focus to understand what's happening to that person and the ability to communicate the meaning of that, and afterwards, for the most part, provides them with ideas of how they can approach something in a surprising manner. It's an additional tool that we have in our toolbox to aid us in wrestling with other people."

Separating It

The Myers-Briggs method can be separated by the following advancements:

* Do you prefer to be focused on the outside world (this is known as extroversion, (or "E") instead of your personal inner the world (introversion or "I")?

* Do you prefer to focus on the most important information you are absorbing (detecting"S" or "S") or do you prefer to understand and add the significance (intuiting"N," or "N")?

* Would you prefer to first look at the rationale and coherence (thinking"T") "T") instead of taking a just take a look at the individual and the unusual conditions when deciding (feeling"F") or "F")?

When you are managing the outside world, do prefer to have things decided (judging or "J") or do you prefer to be open to new ideas and alternative options (seeing"P "P")?

The 16 characters of the MBTI depend on the combination of traits in each class, which is communicated in the four-letter code. Analysts are quick to recognize that there's no perfect type and that the goal of thinking about the character types is to understand and recognize the differences among people. The MBTI doesn't measure characteristics like capacity or character.

A Big Five Journey

Analysts are constantly trying to make character type research more logical. One method to quantify the traits of a person is called"the Big Five (likewise alluded to by the mental aids' CANOE or OCEAN) Receptiveness, good faith, extroversionand appropriateness and neuroticism.

Brian Little, Ph.D. is a member from The Well-Being Institute and chief of the Social Ecology Research Group in the Department of Psychology at Cambridge University. He is the principal researcher about how everyday activities and "free attributes" influence the way our lives, one of the most effective methods of understanding and improving human flourishing.

The event was a continuous One Day University introduction in Dallas, Little utilized an amusing tale to explain the essence of what he called the Big Five character attributes. "Did you know that it's almost impossible for a grownup to touch your elbow's surface?" He asked the crowd. "Also did you realise that your reaction to this information is a clue about your personality?"

Minimal, at this point provided a succinct explanation that followed his OCEAN abbreviation. The main trademark is receptiveness to meet, he explained. "[Those with more openness] are more likely to connect. They look into. They're interested. What do they think they can do with using the elbow as a model? I think they'll be able to try it. Maybe , in a subtle manner, but they're determined to do it."

Being open to interaction can be a good indicator of various successes in daily life, he added particularly in areas that require a creative approach to things that affect us.

The second quality is honesty He also mentioned good faith. "The people who are extremely honest are characterized by a myriad of achievements throughout their lives," he clarified. "Scholastically they will generally achieve better results. In their jobs, they'll generally, possess more efficient methods of execution. They are elevated to higher levels, and perhaps surprisingly, with regard to their physical health, upright individuals beat those who are less faithful.

"Things being the way you are. How will they deal with elbows? Another characteristic is that they're organized, organised. They collaborate. They plot. I doubt they would have done anything to their elbows here. However they might have written an unassuming note that reads"When you return to your home, you should check your the elbow.' "

Minimal was moved towards his E of OCEAN and extroversion. "The one who has left has not only tried or perhaps succeeded in licking their elbows and has also efficiently licked the elbows of the person sitting next theirs," he stated, leading to laughter among the crowd. "Outgoing people like incitement. They love to be occupied with activities that pay off. The more independent person is more reluctant to having done any thing."

Moving on to the A niceties. Little was discussing how the individual could think that it would be nice for the therapist to consider an intricately named process and its dimensions and make them pleasant and relevant to the public by using the elbow account, whereas the person who is not palatable may protest and cite the individual's favorite insight.

Finally, Little was able to move into neurotics in order to finish the OCEAN. "I tend to be more sensitive when talking to people on neuroticism to keep an unintentional distance from the distinctly demeaning character of this term. It is a good idea to talk about extremely, or perhaps overly sensitive persons," he said. "Oversensitivity can cause real discomforts and injuries throughout the course of one's life. People who are hypochondriacs didn't even have any elbow issues However, they did say"Oh my God I've been dreading it for a long period of time I've been detesting the fact I'm not able to rub my elbows, and I think about it after an extended period of time after a the night. Do I have a mental illness? Yes. It's likely."

Putting things in perspective

Little emphasizes that he would not choose any of the Big Five characteristics as fortunate or unfortunate , yet they are distinctive and unique in their own unique way to the challenges people face throughout their daily lives. Mindfulness is the main goal.

"So it could be that there are two aspects to being aware of our own self," Mayer says. "One is understanding how our characters operate and the most important part of that is understanding the elements of character which in the everyday language could be being active or timid and outgoing or shy or trustworthy or numb. If you've got those names, the second step is knowing how and when to apply the words."

Self-information and information about other people is "a combination of your theories possibly of what characters mean and different, and then what you can do to apply those markings to you and others," Mayer says.

The people who know the characters of each other are in a unique favorable place, he claims.

It is also important to be aware of the assertions of experts that just since the world doesn't have high contrast, it doesn't mean that we all are outgoing or self-observers.

"At the point where you buy your Big Five stock, and I'm sure you'll do it you might be in the middle," Little told his One Day University crowd. "The majority of them are in the middle."

These investigations of character allow us to understand what is important to other people and to be able to hear and be aware of the terms they use to be able to effectively speak with them as directed by Nardi.

But, the examination of character is certainly not a book that is closed.

"We clinicians do not have a thorough knowledge of character at the moment," Mayer says. "Various years ago I had done an overview of the character reading materials, and I found that there were over 400 characters which were listed in the glossary in the main textbook. "The Big Five are important things to look over but they are far from the entire important aspects of a person's personality."

Caretaking for Different People

Incoming Sensing (Se)

Incoming Sensing (Se) people perform best when they are in a dynamic environment that is rich in tactile information, with lots of windows, appealing perspectives, and an intriguing style of layout. While working alongside them, provide and stimulate development by using useful breaks like walking groups, strolling and focus on the issues that require the right responses.

Thinkingful Sensing (Si)

In the absence of a sense (Si) people are more prone to low-interruption situations and the opportunity to review events to establish the new knowledge. If you work with them, employ methods that work in a bit-by-bit fashion to aid them in developing abilities, using a roadmap to track progress. think that they should focus on a particular direction or goal longer than you might. Be careful when giving feedback that includes a familiarity with non-verbal signals, such as exterior appearances.

Intelligent Intuiting (Ni)

Chapter 18: Additional Questions To Ask And Things To Avoid

Everyone wants to be an attractive personality that distinguishes you from the crowd. To achieve this, is to be interested and involved in the conversation and also. One of the things you should perform to be a successful conversationalist is to provide your partner with enticing questions that get him talking as well as be a superior listener, and also be capable of asking questions in follow-up that are relevant to the subject. Also, you should be able to bring up the topic to get the juices of a person flowing. Keep the majority of your questions open to allow for natural conversations to take place.

Here are a few examples of intriguing and thought-provoking open-ended questions:

What are you looking for in your life?

What's your objective?

What do you want to see more from your daily life?

What is fun for you? What else?

Are job satisfaction or money the most important thing to you? Why is that?

What do you think about the idea that work and money are connected? What do you think that means for your personal life?

What's stopping you from achieving your goals?

For more questions similar to these check out Tim Hansen's 150 Powerful Question.

Awkward Moment Solutions Awkward Moment Solutions

When you talk to someone you don't are familiar with, it's normal to be awkward for a minute of silence, or even two. To fill in the gap and to stop the person from mumbling "Whelp. We'll see you in a bit," you can use one of these strategies.

1. Setting Set the mood to bring back the discussion. For example, "This place has a nice atmosphere. It's as if we're in Paris. How do you feel about this?" or "That is quite unique artwork displayed on the wall. Are you a fan of artwork?"

The point is that if you're overwhelmed by words, take a look at your surroundings and utilize it to spark the conversation.

2. Compliments: People love compliments. Make sure to praise the person you're speaking with. It's not about complimenting someone on their appearance; I'm talking about complimenting the person on their personality or other things you've noticed in the conversation. One thing to be aware of is that it can cause temporary uncomfortable silence or awkwardness while the person is accepting the compliment. It might be uncomfortable for some people, because many don't know how to acknowledge compliments. The most effective way to acknowledge the compliment is smile, and acknowledge it by saying "thank to you" to avoid awkwardness.

I love using "4 second silence" in which I offer an acknowledgement like "I truly admire you for the fact the fact that you'd give up everything you have in the moment to help homeless people in the street. It shows your appreciation for helping others." Take four seconds for the compliment to be absorbed and for the person to accept it. Afterwards, in case there's no response then start a new conversation.

Themes to Avoid When Talking About Small-Talk

Once you know the topics that are suitable to talk about It is essential to be aware of the topics that are not to be discussed because they can cause conflict and cause the conversation to come at an abrupt end. Some of these subjects may seem obvious, but they need to be addressed. These are the seven subjects to stay clear of during a conversation.

Politics

Different people have their own views regarding politics. You might be speaking to someone who has been a fervent supporter of the politician you dislike. Be careful not to discuss this issue to avoid having both of you to be discussing politics.

Financial Aspect

It's not a good idea to inquire about the financial condition of someone's assets. Business or career of a person is a discussion point but do not inquire about the value in money behind it. People will often feel they are being snubbed.

Religion

This is a delicate subject. Different people have different views regarding the Almighty. If you are averse to the subject, you could cause offence to the person you're speaking to.

Age

It's generally considered rude to request someone's age, especially for women. While most people would divulge their age when they are asked, it's not advised to do so particularly when you first meet anyone.

What is the purpose of asking someone's age? It's not a huge issue.

The most important thing is the way you feel inside. Are you feeling 50 or 25? If you're feeling 50 What are you planning to do to appear younger?

Gossiping

Doing gossip will not make you any friends. Indeed, it could cause you to make enemies. If you for instance you hear from your coworker Betty regarding the way John has been stealing money from the company account, you should not repeat what you heard because John did not inform you of the truth. Betty did.

Perhaps a co-worker John has a relationship with coworker Betty and is looking to inform her of all the negative things that were reported about her. He may know the person who you gossip about personally. Do not talk to people behind their backs.

Avoid Offensive Jokes

It is best to stay clear of offensive jokes (sarcasm that make someone wish to stay away out from others for several days) even if you're trying to add a touch of humor to an event be careful because offensive jokes are more damaging in the event that someone does not have any idea about who you are. They can instantly drop or ruin their initial impression of you. Eventually, they will remember you as "the person who is a jackass and makes offensive jokes" since people are likely to discuss it.

If you do something that is offensive to people around you, you'll be considered to be negative, and the majority of people try their best to avoid people who are negative. If you're looking for methods to create an optimistic mindset go through my book, Positivity.

Sarcasm is acceptable when you know that people who listen to you enjoy these kinds of jokes, like family and friends. Thus, make it an absolute rule not to use humorous, sarcastic jokes that could be offensive. You're not hired to be a comedian and you aren't sure how someone will react.

Chapter 19: Interacting In Group Conversations

In the past, we've dealt on how to effectively communicate in one-on one situations, particularly in the event that you want to improve your social life. You will encounter conversations that are small and how to effectively communicate with others.

In one-on one conversations You:

"* More or less, have the attention of that person

* Are able to have deeper conversations

* You only need to create a positive impression with that person

• Have greater control over the direction you're able to guide the conversation

Conversations in groups do not happen in this manner, and, naturally, it's natural for extroverts to get up in these situations. Situations of socializing in groups can be exhausting and stressful, particularly for introverts. It is tempting to avoid them, however they are just as effective in improving your communication skills as individual interactions.

Before we dive into the advantages of socializing with others Let's look at the reasons why people are uneasy in large groups.

It is possible to feel unimportant and may be unable to make meaningful connections during the period of time. In a large group it can be difficult to get your voice into the conversation, especially if there's one person who is the center of attention and draws all attention to them. The act of speaking up can be difficult, especially if the conversation is noisy and chaotic.

Sometimes, the issues lie with the topic being debated. It might not be something you are familiar with, so naturally it is unlikely that you'll be able to make a contribution effectively.

It is also possible that it's the type of situation in a group that's daunting to you. It could be that the event isn't suited to your strengths in social interaction or personal style. There are many kinds of events for groups. There are some that are energetic and loud which is where an extrovert could be more at their element. These kinds of group interactions require individuals to show more confidence when it comes to communicating. While this may appear to be unorthodox in other situations, it's acceptable and is even expected in these situations. If you're too soft-spoken in this instance, you'll be ignored and be get lost among the other people.

The other kinds of events are more sombre and more reserved, where people who are introverted may feel more at ease. When you attend these occasions, people aren't as eager to take the spotlight. You are not required to assert yourself to assert your right to be a part of the conversation. to the discussion.

There is also the kind of people at the event. These may not be the people that you are accustomed to This makes communication challenging.

The way you conduct yourself at gatherings has a large amount to do with how you interact with others. If you don't want to attend the event and you don't want to be there, it's going to be a painful experience for you.

So, it is important to be aware that some group events might appeal to you however, others might not be. Also, there's no reason to make a decision in this case. Choose the events in your group which are most suitable for you and then attend these events more than other events. Whatever group activities you go to it is essential to possess certain traits to succeed in the group interaction.

Conclusion

Maybe chatting with a new classmate prior to your lecture about your instructor or the book you were chosen to read the previous week could bring about a new relationship. Engaging in a conversation during the lunch hour with that guy who is sitting across from yourself at the restaurant's sushi restaurant could result in a fresh job or business partnership. Perhaps that person was able to make a decision to invest in a flimsy idea you talked about with him you've been contemplating realizing it, but you didn't have the money to support it. This won't occur if you spend all the time gazing at the straw of your beverage cup all time, because you're afraid to be involved.

The wait of two hours at the DMV might not be longer when you're engaging in conversation with the lady beside you, waiting for her number be called. Even if you do not ever see her again the next day, the bond and the small talk have fulfilled its purpose. A uncomfortable and painful experience transformed into a pleasant one through a simple conversations.

If we don't let something odd or unusual hinder us from taking advantage of a possible chance, we are engaging in conversation with an open mind , and making ourselves ready to have a great conversation which could be the start of something much bigger and more rewarding. Conversation with a stranger could be as simple as conversing with anyone else. If you and the other engage in a conversation that is interesting to both of you and get comfortable with each and each other, conversations can be fluid and effortless. Making sure you ask the right open-ended questions, and offering answers that may bring about further discussion are two ways of actively seeking to create something more than informal conversation. Be sure to follow through in what you tell people you're planning to say is another method of building confidence with someone who might have begun as an unwelcome visitor. If you put in an effort and showing that you care, even something that started as small talk could be a success if handled correctly.

The process of making a connection with a stranger can be very easy to do. With all the different aspects that catch your attention it is likely that you will discover at least one thing that you have in the same with someone you're speaking to. In the simplest sense what is the reason for you having the same environment? Everyone would like to make connections and feel comfortable in our own environment and with people we have no idea or not. Small talk can serve to help accomplish this and more. However, nothing can be accomplished if you're shy to talk first, and then talk to others, or even engage. Each time you choose to be quiet is a chance lost and you've missed the chance to gain knowledge, discover something new, meet someone, or anyone else, since the possibilities that are available through a small talk can be endless depending on who you're speaking to and what you're discussing.

The conversation may not produce something more than that, and after taking the time necessary to engage in an informal conversation, you may realize that you don't need to continue it, even. But the right conversation can lead to the

www.ingramcontent.com/pod-product-compliance
Lightning Source LLC
Chambersburg PA
CBHW050409120526
44590CB00015B/1896